what lurks at the bottom of my PANTY DRAWER

Lessons I've Learned from Kiddos, Critters, and Coochies

By Kasey Brooks

authorHOUSE®

AuthorHouse™ LLC
1663 Liberty Drive
Bloomington, IN 47403
www.authorhouse.com
Phone: 1-800-839-8640

Published by AuthorHouse   01/20/2014

ISBN: 978-1-4918-0733-0(sc)
ISBN: 978-1-4918-0732-3 (e)

Library of Congress Control Number: 2013914862

This book is printed on acid-free paper.

DEDICATION

My memoir about the goofy lessons life has taught me—the hard way, is dedicated to my husband who helps me see the silver lining through our crazy adventures and who accepts me for the quirky, passionate, strange, and often irrational person that I am. It is also dedicated to my two children, the true teachers of the bizarre lessons life throws at me. And finally, to my grandparents who are my eternal cheerleaders, and to my mom who has the biggest heart in the world.

ACKNOWLEDGMENTS

I would like to give a big shout-out to the special people in my life who have made the last few years survivable and who have kept me from sticking my head in the oven. A huge thank you to my sweet husband who has been a wonderful pseudo-mom to our kids when I needed to sit in front of the computer and type ad nauseam; also, thank you for putting up with my meltdowns and tantrums that occurred whenever a deadline loomed. Thank you to my grandmother who is my wise encourager and to my late grandfather for instilling the importance of education. Thank you to my mom, Sharon, who picked her battles while I was growing up so I could blossom into the quirky person I am today. And to my mother-in-law, Janise, who entertains my kids while I am buried in paperwork. Thank you to Folgers coffee for helping me survive two and a half years with very little sleep. A big hug to my friends who have proofread my stories and shared their opinions toward my writing endeavor, especially to Rachel Hartig, and the Fearsome Foursome who've kidnapped me for coffee breaks and cheered me on through the challenging times. Thanks to the fabulous Andi Artze of 2A Photography for taking my author picture, to Staci McKinnon (my brilliant muse) who encourages me to dream "beyond just hardwood floors", and to the extraordinarily talented Christie Skinner who designed the front cover that perfectly captures my life. And a humongous thanks to Dr. Sarah Wakefield for tirelessly editing my work and offering fabulous ideas and suggestions to make my writing sparkle. I could not have done any of this without y'all! Finally, a special thanks to those taking the time out of your crazy-busy schedule to read this; I appreciate you, and in return, I hope I can give you a few giggles.

CONTENT

Introduction xi

1.   Lust at First Sight 1
2.   My Guardian Angel's Blueprint 5
3.   Oh, Crap! 9
4.   An Eye for an Eye, a Tooth for a Tooth 12
5.   Pride: A Terrible Thing to Waste 14
6.   Je Suis Idiote! 18
7.   Nipples in the Neighborhood 21
8.   Coochie Conundrums 25
9.   Ancestral 'Roots' 29
10. Just Because You Can Swallow,
     Doesn't Mean You Should 32
11. Out of the Mouths of ~~Babes~~ Grandmothers 35
12. Does Size Really Matter? 38
13. Permanent Scars: Tats Vs. Teenagers 41
14. Hip, Jazz-Hands, Pose ... and Blush 43
15. Attention Sales Associates: Clean-Up on Aisle Two 45
16. Umm ... I Think You've Seen My Vagina 47
17. Dang Homonyn: The Clan Vs. The Klan 50
18. Alert: Creeper at the Pool! 53
19. White Icing Vs. White Lies 57
20. Sex-Mail Slip-Up 59
21. You Can Suck on Me Any Time 61
22. What Lurks at the Bottom of the Panty Drawer 63
23. Burning Ring of Fire 68
24. Don't Judge a Book by Its Cover 71
25. Burned Retinas 73
26. Getting Suckered Sucks 76
27. Wine Me, Dine Me ... But Now the Party's Over 85

28. Phallic Fallacy...87
29. Kids Don't Just Suck Your Boob,
    They Suck Your Self-Esteem...........................89
30. I Understand Why AnimalsEat Their Offspring...........91
31. Got Milk?...99
32. Open Mouth, Insert Foot................................101
33. Pi Is to Be Eaten,Not Calculated! 106
34. Junk in the Trunk.......................................109
35. Out of the Mouths of Babes............................112
36. Webster: You're Needed in Room 120 113
37. Who's the A**hole Now? 115
38. "Hi-Ya!" ... "Hi-Oww!" 117
39. The Butt of the Joke...................................119
40. I Give Up ... Eat Like a Slob!.......................122
41. My Genes for My Jeans Suck............................123
42. To Thong or Not to Thong ... That Is the Question......125
43. Show-and-Tell Needs a Translator......................129
44. CTRL + ALT + DELETE....................................132
45. Add This Event to My Daughter's
    Future Therapy Bill....................................134
46. Piggy Porn 136
47. "Ladies and Gents—Step Right Up to the
    Freak Show in Cage 3" 141
48. Purse-gasm 142
49. Quite the Charmer.......................................146
50. May I Buy You a ... Car Wash?..........................148
51. They All Look Alike to Me 150
52. Shove That Cookie Where the Sun Don't Shine! 152
53. Hotter Than a Hooker at Church.........................156
54. The Metaphorical "Kid".................................158
55. I'm Proud of My Fourth Grade Prostitute 160
56. This Requires How Much Butter? 163
57. Sweating in Hell but Hoping for Heaven 165
58. Oh, Goodness Snakes Alive!............................167
59. May I Just Lick You So It'll Rub Off On Me? 169
60. Woman of the Evening....................................171
61. He Ain't ~~Heavy~~ Gummy,He's My Brother 174
62. What's Your Emergency?.................................176

63. Work It, Girl (Scout) 178
64. Welcome to the Neighborhood! 180
65. Don't Make Me Hurt You..182
66. Don't Hassle the Hound..184
67. If You Can't Fix Crazy, You Can at
    Least Clean It First...188
68. Mistaken for a Pawn Star 189
69. Mum's the Word..191
70. The Event in My Life That'll Earn Me a
    Shiny Crown in Heaven 194
71. Peeking Buns Preventing Peking Duck....................198

Conclusions...201

INTRODUCTION

We all wear masks to cover up how we truly feel inside. We put on our figurative sexy panties to show our more attractive traits, but it's often a smokescreen. What lurks at the bottom of who we truly are is often filled with rips, stretched elastic, and discoloration, just like our old comfy pair of disheveled panties we hide from the public eye. We smile at others through clenched teeth, use our manners when we really want to punch someone in the trachea, and allow the words, "Sure, I can volunteer for that," when really all we want to do is crawl in a hole and hibernate away from the commitments we pile on ourselves through guilt, the desire to please others, and wanting to feel accepted.

This collection of humorous, autobiographical memoirs exposes my *real* life—the life I try to make perfectly pretty on the outside with fabulous stilettos, loads of mascara, and exquisite purses. Yet, underneath the façade, I'm barely hanging on to the scraps life throws at me.

Each of the stories included in this book have taught me some sort of life lesson—some silly and some poignant. But each lesson helps remove the top layer of beautiful "panties" I want others to think I'm wearing and really digs to the bottom of the "drawer" to discover the true me. The me that's flawed and a bit stained from the crap life throws at us.

Lust at First Sight

The eccentric author Truman Capote once explained in a television interview that the closest sensation to an orgasm is a sneeze. I beg to differ. The closest sensation to an orgasm is purchasing a new purse. Not just any purse, but *the* purse. You know the one—way too freaking expensive. The kind that makes you actually consider feeding your children peanut butter and noodles for a month just so your shoulder can support that new, perfectly-pocketed, sensational-smelling, leather purse.

Each year, my girlfriends and I meet up three hours away at a huge outlet mall in San Marcos, Texas. This is the kind of place that takes twelve hours, if you estimate conservatively, to plow through every store. If we take a wish list and divide-and-conquer, we can tear that place apart in ten hours if some good coffee is involved.

One shopping weekend, the top item on my list happens to be a snake-skin purse. I want the real-deal: nothing plastic, nothing fabric, nothing shiny. I want scales. Scales may make most women shiver in disgust. To me, they are foreplay leading up to the ultimate purse-gasm.

Twelve hours pass … yet my conquest still isn't crossed off my list. I'm bummed, but at 8PM, my friend Michelle and I need to get on the road to head back to Houston. Three hours to drive back to the Space City, plus our traditional hour of getting lost in Austin, puts us in right at midnight. Michelle knows me well enough to see I've left the outlet unsatisfied and wanting more. Those knock-off purses have only flirted with me or bought me the proverbial drink. And a few have even gotten to second base. None have hit that homerun I so desperately need.

Michelle pulls off the road and into a parking lot. I inquire, "Where are we going?" She responds, "Dillard's. We can't leave without checking a department store for that dang reptile bag."

Searching the purses before closing time, I now know how a desperate man at a bar feels right before they announce, "Last call!" Just as he roams the rows of bar stools for that one face that might be "the one," I'm doing the same with the handbags, feeling them up with my eyes.

At 8:32, the perfect 10 makes its appearance. This purse is hotter than David Beckham. Sexier than Brad Pitt. More smoldering than Bradley Cooper. The purse is a Brahmin (a high-end, handcrafted luxury line, for the bag-benighted).

I give it the eye. I blush. I grope it with intensity, hoping it feels the electricity in my fingertips like I sense the sparks in its 100% genuine animal skin. It yearns for me. We have chemistry. The only way I can take it home and have my way with it is to try it on for a while, press it against my body, and let it rest against the curve of my waist.

Walking around the store with it on my shoulder until 8:58, I have to make a decision: pay the $400 or gain some self-control, restrain my lust, choose my children's nutrition over the purse.

The leather goddess wins.

No, it wasn't the snakeskin I was searching for, but sometimes, what you want and what your body needs are two different things. It is an alligator bag big enough to make my butt look small in comparison. And it's all mine, darlin'.

I need to make a confession. Hello, my name is Kasey Brooks, and I'm addicted to Brahmin. Their handbags are timeless, well-constructed pieces of leather art. Since that magical day, I save my money for twelve months to buy just one new purse at our annual shopping trip. They ain't cheap, honey!

The first twelve months tick away slowly, but it's now time for our annual trip to the outlets. Apparently, every other suburban mom has the same plan as we sit in traffic by the entrance for forty-five sweaty minutes in the month of May. Why is everyone here? Don't they know I want to do our traditional shopping all day long and then run to Dillard's again at 8PM to search for another Brahmin to satiate my sweet spot?

Mother's Day weekend. GetoutofmywayskanksIneedto shop!

Inching up to where we can see the mall but were still about ¼ mile away, I see it! The Heavens open. The angels blow the trumpet. THIS IS THE DAY! Brahmin has opened up an outlet store in the mall! Cheaper prices mean last year's model, but who cares! The passion overtakes me. My heart races. My breathing is erratic. I'm sweating—and not just because it's bikini weather in Texas. I have to break free from this metal box holding my lust bridled.

Swinging open the door, I escape. I briskly walk down the side of the freeway, but as the sign grows bigger, I can't get to it fast enough. I'm in a full-out sprint as my friends are leaning out the car window, hollering, "Kasey, what are you doing?" All I could do it point, pant, and run.

I arrive at last at the gates of handbag-Heaven that bid me to enter. St. Peter greets me and guides me by the arm to enter the land of bliss (actually, he is the gay manager, Sebastian, who now knows me on a first-name basis and sends me personal emails when sales approach at his store). Then and there, it hit me.

Purse-gasm.

I moan in delight. I shriek. I squeal. My eyes roll around in my head.

I.Can't.Get.Enough.

I.Can't.Get.Enough.Oxygen.

Whew.

Satisfied, I walk through the bounty of beautiful Brahmins, stroking each one with caresses of tender affection. And this is how my love affair begins ...

Lesson Learned: You'll never forget your first time. Ahh ...

My Guardian Angel's Blueprint

Do you ever feel the universe conspires with all of its elements to stop you from doing something it knows you shouldn't do? I can just picture a huge boardroom in the sky: my guardian angel sits there, Karma perched on his left and Catastrophe on his right planning to sabotage upcoming events to coerce me toward making different decisions or to warn me of impending doom. I'm convinced this is precisely what happened in regard to my *first* wedding day.

Many people ask me how my husband Tom and I met. We first dated in college when I was nineteen. However, when I turned twenty, I stupidly married someone else. The old adage is so painfully true: hindsight is 20/20. Actually, hindsight is 20/10 with a good Lasik procedure. If I could go back in time, I'd ask myself these questions: Why on earth did you get married at age 20? To a narcissist? To a cheater? To someone with an addictive personality? And to someone seen around Houston dressed in drag? Seriously?

How do smart girls end up making dumb choices? I know my angel must follow me around, holding up symbolic neon signs saying "Do Not Enter" while throwing blockades along my path. My celestial being must have been exhausted by the time he lost his fight with my I-know-what-I'm-doing-because-I'm-a-twenty-year-old-who-can't-be-told-what-to-do battle-of-the-wills.

I should have known just from the proposal process that something was awry. Carter, the proposer. Carter was awry.

When he silently passed me the cloudiest diamond on the planet during a commercial break watching a Houston

Rockets basketball game, I should have seen the light or at least a blinking neon sign. Not exactly romantic or heartfelt.

At every turn, disaster sought me out, begging me to turn back before my August wedding date to Carter. The florist packed up and moved out of town two weeks before my big day. The cake showed up to the reception entirely wrong. The looney-tunes mother-in-law-to-be Babs waltzed in wearing the same dress as my bridesmaids. And my father-in-law, Sal ... oh, wow.

Sal was injured a week before the wedding after tumbling down stairs at a baseball stadium. He broke numerous bones in his body and spent the next seven days in-and-out of consciousness in intensive care. Since Carter and Babs didn't want Sal to miss his only child's nuptials, they hired an ambulance service to transport a moaning Sal down the aisle. The EMT workers' orange jumpsuit uniforms didn't exactly match the tuxes and dresses. However, Sal *did* match the color theme of black and red because Babs thoughtfully wrapped him like a mummy in *black* bed sheets. His squeaking gurney was wheeled down the center aisle and parked by the pulpit to serve his role as the best man, even though he wasn't awake. To all the three hundred guests, he appeared deceased, like the ambulance made a pit stop to pick up a dead body before arriving at the church.

We said our vows, which apparently had a five-year expiration date, and proceeded back down the aisle. As the groomsmen recess, Craig, who had just been diagnosed with the flu, fainted and conked his head against an old woman's face in the audience. Luckily, the ambulance workers were there to work their magic with Craig's unconscious body in the middle of the aisle and the woman's eye whose eyeglasses cut her face.

Throughout the reception the groom constantly rolled his eyes expressing his annoyance at the whole wedding ordeal. Nothing's more nostalgic than a photo album of a smiling bride and an eye-rolling groom.

Normally, grooms want to leave and get to the hotel to get down-and-dirty with the bride. Not this groom. After I changed into a beautiful, white negligee beaded with pearls and crystals, he announced he preferred to watch the hockey game on TV. I slinked off to sleep—alone and untouched.

Even the animals on our non-erotic honeymoon tried to warn me. Carter thought it would be fun to go on a fishing vacation. Fishing for a week? To celebrate our marriage? Nothing is less sexy than slimy fish scales and impaling worms on the end of a rusty hook. The fish refused to bite … and pathetically, so did Carter.

Taking a break from the water for a few hours, we headed out west to a drive-thru animal safari. Offering tasty niblets to the animals while hanging out the car window proved to be dangerous as an antelope charged and attacked my arms with his horns. Bleeding, I ducked back into my seat, defeated by nature and ready to head back to the fishing cabin to put on some comfy ~~lingerie~~ sweatpants.

The honeymoon and the next five years are more of the same: one catastrophe after another and without much nookie to make up for it. I knew the marriage needed to end after a brutal fight and Sal coming over to confess Carter had been having affairs. Affairs with men. Affairs with women. Affairs with whoever could feed his ego.

My dachshund solidified this finale by peeing inside Carter's baseball hat. As he left the house, Carter popped on his trusty ol' hat as dog dittle ran all down his handsome, self-absorbed little face. At this moment, I can picture my angel invisibly giving the dog a good belly rub and saying, "Finally! Now, let's get Kasey to Tom, the true love of her life."

We reconnect. And I live happily ever after with my quality-diamond-buying, hockey-hating, sex-loving, non-narcissistic Tom.

Lesson Learned: Sometimes life has to slap you silly before you become aware of the blessings God is preparing for you. When catastrophes hit one after another, take a moment to reflect and listen for the flutter of wings trying to work their magic by waving a neon orange detour sign in front of your nose.

Oh, Crap!

The two years between my divorce from my first husband (the narcissistic drag queen), and my marriage to my forever husband, Tom, I was single and ready to mingle. I knew that after being married to someone more obsessed with the label on a designer handbag than I was, that I wanted to find a manly-man. Someone who couldn't care less about purses. Someone who has nice calluses on his hands. Someone who can change the oil in his car without worrying about his hair getting messed up. And frankly, someone who can get it on in the sack without having to have the lights out and alcohol involved to even approach my girly-parts. I'm a southern girl who wants a strong southern man. A horse wouldn't be a bad addition either.

I'm not trying to reinforce the stereotype that every family owns a horse in Texas, but if you don't own one personally, then you probably have a family member who does. My uncle and aunt board their Quarter-Horse at some really nice stables; I enjoy walking up and down the rows of stalls and viewing the names of the owners etched on the wooden gates. Many of the names are recognizable from influential and wealthy Houston families. Bingo. A potential cowboy with a few extra bucks in his Wranglers!

Along with boarding their horse here, my relatives receive free horseback riding lessons. Not needing new riding techniques for themselves, they offer the lessons to me. I'll take 'em. I'm on a mission.

Putting on my typical Texas-chick make-up (way-too-shiny lip gloss and enough mascara to look like two tarantulas doing the tango on my eyelids), I tease my hair just the right amount, buckle on my rhinestone belt, head out to ride that horse and find me a cute bronco-buster.

Prepping a horse to ride, especially in the summer Texas heat, is not glamorous. It is sweaty, dirty, and quite stinky. Finally my mighty steed Fritz is all set to go, so I swing my leg over the top of him in a very Debra Winger-from-the-movie-*Urban Cowboy*-kind-of-way.

Off I ride, trying to suck in every jiggle and ripple of divorce pounds I have gained. After forty-five minutes, I call it quits. Horse hair keeps getting stuck in my lip gloss and I fear butt-sweat is about to rear its ugliness in my jeans, so I decide it is time for Fritz to get his bath and rest.

I've always been somewhat intrigued by music videos with a seductive carwash scene. Since the horse needs a good hosing down, I think to myself, "Hmm. I can sooo spray him down in a rock-goddess kind of way." Wrong. Spraying down an uncooperative, sweaty horse is nothing at all like spraying down a shiny, red Corvette. There's nothing remotely sexy about it, unfortunately.

After combing his mane, feeding him carrots, cleaning coagulated poop from the hooves, and wiping the torrential downpour of sweat from my brow, I put him up in his stall.

I saunter over and try to make small talk with guys at the stables. Yet, they completely blow me off. One guy tips his hat, shakes his head, and walks away. The other gives me a quick glance, adjusts himself in his Wranglers, and dismisses me like he does the tobacco juice he squirts from his mouth.

Hellooo?! What's happened to southern manners in front of a lady? I can't figure it out. Not that I'm God's gift to cowboys, but seriously, I'm rockin' these jeans!

Yanking off my spurs, I shake my boots off before climbing into my car and reach up for my sunglasses I'd hooked on to the rearview mirror. It takes less than half a second to comprehend why I was receiving zero attention from the horse dudes. In horror and disgust, I shout, "Oh, crap!"

Literally. My forehead is smeared from one side to the other side with fresh horse doody. No amount of lip gloss, teased Texas hair, or sexy jeans can distract men from smeared manure on a woman's face.

Note to Self: When cleaning horse hooves, use a bandana to wipe your brow, not your dirty hands. Or at least check yourself in a shiny, reflective belt buckle before making a stinkin' fool of yourself.

Lesson Learned: Through our struggle to acquire outward attention through beauty, we're all smeared with a little bit of pony poop. Wipe it off and move on with life.

An Eye for an Eye, a Tooth for a Tooth

For my cousin's wedding, my mother, whom I call the Martha Stewart of Texas, puts together the cute party favors that will sit at each place setting on the reception tables: beautiful boxes origamied into elegant shapes filled with white candied-coated almonds and topped-off with a sentimental message attached by an iridescent ribbon.

Months after the wedding, she still has mounds of leftover candy in these cute boxes, since she'd bought them in bulk. While I am chilling at her house and having a good chat with my grandmother, they try to pawn off some of the leftover almonds. Grandmothers are not truly happy unless they are shoving food in your face. Not being one to pass up sugar in any form, I gladly accept.

I've learned the hard way that while eating these almonds, you have to suck on them first. Biting straight into them is begging for an emergency trip to the dentist, so from experience, I know to work on each individual nut patiently.

I pop the next one in my mouth, which is rounder than the usual cylindrical shape. After sucking off the candy coating, I try to bite into the almond, which by this point is usually softened somewhat. Yet, it won't budge.

Complaining to my mom about the candy's refusal to mush, I continue to work on the almond. Finally, a crunch occurs! After the nut refuses to crumble and feeling shocks of discord on my own teeth, I give up and pull it out of my mouth.

No wonder I can't crush it. It's a human tooth! For the last ten minutes, I have been sucking on a human tooth masquerading as an elegant candy-coated almond! Gag.

Lesson Learned: Never throw away the original container until the food is completely consumed. To the factory worker who is missing his tooth, I have it for you ... for a small reward. And, no. The tooth fairy didn't come when I put it under my pillow. It was worth a try.

Pride: A Terrible Thing to Waste

The weather in Houston is incredibly unpredictable, and so are the football teams. It can be one hundred and three degrees outside with clear, sunny skies, and within ten minutes, it'll drop twenty degrees as hurricane force winds descend and a flash flood creeps up your ankles. It's just the same in football. One minute your team is on top of the ranking, and the next minute, you are second to last. I can fully relate.

When I began to teach in the public school sector, part of my contract stated I also had to be the cheerleading coach of the junior high squad. Yes, even though I was never a cheerleader, I guess a college degree in dance covered the qualifications. I'm convinced they rope in inexperienced 23-year-old teachers who are desperate for a job and are fit enough to not break a hip while spotting seventh graders on top of a topsy-turvy pyramid. So, I signed my name on the contract and warmed up my pom-poms.

That year, the Panthers are surprisingly ranked number one in the district, which means we'll be competing against the Eagles in the play-offs at the arena where the high schoolers normally play their games. This stadium is quite large for a high school facility, so you can imagine how excited the cheerleaders, players, coaches, parents, students, and administrators are about playing the championship game at this location: big stuff for a seventh grade team!

To boost the spirit of the players and show our Panther pride, my cheerleaders paint five purple and white ten-foot banners that we secure with duct tape onto the brick walls of the opposing side of the stadium so our fans could clearly see them from across the field. We spend days painting these dang banners with slogans like "Poach the Eagles!" and, "Annihilate the Nest!"

All is going smoothly. The megaphones are all lined up in perfect formation, the duct tape is adhering securely to the brick wall, my principal is there sitting next to me to do my yearly evaluation of my cheerleading coaching abilities to put in my 'permanent record' (does anyone know if that 'record' even really exists?). Most importantly, I have on a new purple outfit that I purchased specifically to show my Purple Panther Pride: a silk, sleeveless blouse that tucks into a silk wrap-around skirt that ties at the hip in a perfect, but not too bunchy, bow. Yep, I'm rockin' it.

Silk is a tricky fabric to wear. It's feminine, classy, and has just the right amount of cling, without showing too much body shape, especially while teaching junior high boys ... ick. However, the big problem with this type of style is that panty lines look like they have taken illegal steroids and have multiplied with a raging vengeance across the butt. Therefore, I decide to forego panties that day (which is something I rarely ever do, I promise!) and just depend upon my diligence in always making sure the skirt is discreetly pulled down and my knees always "hit the cymbals," as my sister says in reference to crossing one's legs. Call me crazy, but I'd rather go commando than show panty lines to the world, which completely ruins the effect of a cute new outfit. Don't judge.

All is going well so far: none of the cheerleaders has obtained a concussion, their crazy moms who live vicariously through their drama-filled daughters are staying away from my bleacher, and our team is winning. What could possibly go wrong? Oh, yes. I forgot. Houston weather.

Suddenly and without warning, the wind picks up. My sweet-but-scary principal opens his mouth to talk to me and the wind catches hold of his jowls in quite a phenomenal way. His cheeks look like a Basset Hound's mouth running through a field of clover. I squint to avoid losing a contact lens in the wind just in time to lean closer and hear him say, "Look at the sky!" Either God is a Purple Panther fan Himself, or the purple clouds are about to dump a torrential downpour right on top of our painted spirit banners and my new silk outfit. The referees, using their lightning detectors, are forced to call off the game. Using all my weight and muscle, I strain against the wind to make my way down to the field and to the opposing side's brick wall to take down our banners and gather the pom-poms we use as décor.

As the crowd gives a rowdy round of applause to our exiting football players for taking the lead in what little game they played, I rip down all five banners in a hurry and twirl them up in my arms. With banners filling my arms and covering my face, I can only see the ground directly below me, as I realize one of my cheerleaders has inadvertently dropped one of the pom-poms. I dutifully squat down with the "cymbals" still connected to retrieve the orphaned pom-pom just as a gust of wind catches my silk-no-panty-wearing-wrap-around-skirt and flings it outward like a super-hero's cape for the entire stadium to witness. Here I stand: face covered with a banner, pom-poms in hand, and my bare fuzzy biscuit for two hundred bystanders to witness.

My savior, the sixty-year-old principal, bolts down the stadium stairs as fast as his arthritic legs can carry him and hobbles across the field. He instinctively grabs the two sides of my outstretched skirt and wraps them back around my legs. Together, with Mr. Woods (no pun intended with his name and how up close and personal he had to get to help me) holding my skirt closed, and me with my dang pom-poms and banners, we waddle like two connected ducks across the field, much to my horrific dismay.

I did receive an outstanding evaluation from him that school year. I'll never be sure if I truly did a good job at teaching my seventh grade English classes and controlling fourteen junior high cheerleaders and their wacko moms, or if he just felt sorry for me … or if he liked what he saw.

Lesson Learned: If you are going to showcase your lady parts to a stadium full of people, at least make sure you have been warding off cellulite with plenty of squats. On second thought, always wear undergarments and display those panty lines with pride, sister!

Je Suis Idiote!

My grandparents have always said they would rather see our family enjoy our inheritance from them while they are still alive. So, their enjoyment is spending some of their money on family vacations. Hooray- we're heading to Europe! With our over-sized, red matching suitcases for all thirteen of us, we parade through England, Scotland, and France. I should have known at that point what the potential for public humiliation might be.

I have just finished my college degrees in English and Dance Education when we go to England. While in London, we have a free afternoon with no tours scheduled, so we each decide to do our own thing. I am currently teaching English as my day job, while dancing with a modern dance company in the evenings and weekends. Dance is where I find my groove. Literally and figuratively.

There is a famous dance studio in London called The Pineapple, where many famous dancers rehearse in the daytime, especially those performing in traveling Broadway shows. At The Pineapple during the time frame when I'm visiting, a famous choreographer from Paris is scheduled to be a guest teacher. This is huge for me!

London + The Pineapple + Famous Teacher= SCORE!

My mom decides to go with me. She says she wants to see what it's like, but now that I look back, I'm positive it is because I'm geographically challenged, and she knows I will get lost, end up in the dungeon of the Tower of London and never be heard from again. Probably accurate.

We arrive. I pay my class fee and begin warming up my muscles in the back corner of the studio. As I look around,

I realize quickly that modern dance class in the USA is very different from modern dance class in the UK in that we dance barefooted here in the States, while they wear shoes in Europe. I'm surprised and definitely unprepared. Quickly, I learn the reason why they wear shoes when I feel the sharp stings of splinters piercing my feet. The floors in their dance studios aren't smooth and finished; instead, they are rough and don't hesitate to rip up the soles of the bare feet.

The snooty little French choreographer sashays in the studio with an arrogant air like he is some kind of royalty descended directly from King Louis XIV, the creator of ballet. Applause erupts from all of his adoring pupils as he snaps his overly-manicured fingers to signal the beginning of our overly-priced lesson.

Much to my surprise, flashes start going off from the corner of the room. For a moment, I wonder if a newspaper reporter is there to take a few snapshots and write a piece on this high-falutin dance teacher. The flashes continue, and yes, are annoying and quite distracting. I turn my head to check it out. It's my mother snapping picture after picture of me, much to my horror! The whole ordeal would be perfect for that TV show about pageant kids performing on cue with wacked-out stage moms; however, I'm 25 years old! Lovely, Mom. Add this to my therapy bill.

The camera catches the teacher's attention. Seeing the camera is pointed directly at me, he flounces over to stop the commotion and then notices my feet. With his nose in the air and his buns squeezed tightly in white leggings that only Baryshnikov can truly pull off well, he glares at me up and down with a smirk on his face that looks like he had just sucked a lemon. He pauses for dramatic effect and asks in his French accent, "Where are your shoes?"

My heart races as all eyes from the professional Broadway dancers drill disgusted looks at me. Yet, my mother keeps flashing pictures like she is a paparazzo. Afraid to speak and trying to hide the pain from the splinters in my feet, the most redneck, back-woods, podunk accent you've ever heard escapes my mouth as I respond, "We don't wear shoes in Texas."

Seriously, Kasey? "We don't wear shoes in Texas"? Congratulations for just confirming the stereotype of Texans: hicks who ride horses everywhere we go with our huge cowboy hat while roping cattle ... probably barefooted.

Mr. Twinkle-Toes crinkles his nose, turns on his heel, and points at me to get in the back line of the class. Look, I'm proud to be a native Texan, but at this moment, I want to dig a hole in that splintery wooden floor and keep digging until I arrive safely back in Houston where my accent will be fully appreciated.

At the end of the class, I fully realize I have grown up in the typical American home where my talent is praised far higher than it should have been in comparison to these pros. As part of her maternal duty, Mom buys me a t-shirt from The Pineapple as a souvenir. Personally, I think the splinters and the hit to my pride are enough of a take home reminder.

Lesson Learned: As I reflect, I pledge to never be ashamed to have a Texas accent ever again ... even in front of the French who sound like they constantly have a big, green loogie stuck in the back of their throats. Choke on that.

Nipples in the Neighborhood

I struggle with saying the word no. I fully intend to pronounce the 'n' sound, but the word yes suddenly escapes my lips without warning. So when Suzanne asked me to dog-sit her 160 pound Newfoundland for the weekend, I complied. After all, this friend helped me get through my divorce and her husband crafted my legal documents free of charge. How could I utter the word no?

Here I am—a single girl on the cusp of her thirties on a Friday night wiping dog drool off my chin. Hey, I'm not complaining. It's the only tongue I've gotten in a long time. And at this juncture in my life, dogs are more loyal than men. Just me, Winston, and a movie from Suzanne's stash I pop into the machine. What could be sexier?

With my head resting on a hairy canine belly, I watch in awe as Angela Bassett in *What's Love Got to Do with It* shimmies and shakes her groove thang in the role of Tina Turner. How does she gyrate without an ounce of jiggle in her junk? No ripple in her thighs as she dances in revealing costumes. No bounce or bobble anywhere on her bod.

This gets me thinking. My legs are my best asset, so how much movement can I perform in front of a mirror without any sway of cellulite? Hey—don't judge. It's a weekend. I'm single without prospects. I'm mind-numbingly bored. Bring on the leg-jiggle experiment.

I wiggle out of my pajama pants leaving my white tank top and purple thong to expose my physique. With the dance scene of "Proud Mary" cued, I take my pose on the stage bed in front of the mirror and Winston. Singing at the top of my lungs, I vibrate, tremor, and quiver, throwing my arms up-

and-over my head as my feet stomp a motion that resembles walking on hot coals.

My canine companion stares in confusion, perking his ears and cocking his head from right to left. I realize Suzanne must never behave in such a way as Winston gets up and hides in another room.

The experiment concludes. Angela Bassett—you're a no-jiggle-goddess, and I'm your underling. I bow to your firm thighs and tight tushy cheeks. I finish the movie and fall asleep in defeat.

I wake up to Winston whining by the backdoor. 6AM? Seriously? On a Saturday? Still in my lack-of-clothing from last night, I roll out of bed and accompany the dog onto the patio. The door latches behind me as I realize … I'm locked out.

Are. You. Freaking. Kidding. Me?!

With a leftover bobby pin in my hair, I try to pick the lock.

Nada.

Hiding in the bushes, I make my way to the front yard and pray to God that a window will be unlatched.

No dice.

Two hours go by in the July heat with the dog panting in his fur-coat and me sitting on the hot concrete with tiny rocks perforating my bare buns. Just when I think I've hit rock-bottom, the lawn crew opens the back gate ready to mow Suzanne's lawn.

Just four men who don't speak English and me—wearing not much more than a humiliated grin.

I have two choices: 1) Have these dudes gawk at me until they finish the lawn and wait till Suzanne gets back home that night, surviving dehydration from a rusty water spigot, or 2) Go to the neighbor's house and ask to borrow the phone.

I don't want to be medically responsible for their eyes popping out of their skull in dirty adoration, so I back out of the yard face-forward hiding my bare booty. I mosey my way out the gate and into the neighbor's yard just as the sprinkler system activates. White tank top and water? The nipplage leaves nothing to the imagination.

This is every lawn man's wet dream.

And my wet nightmare.

I ring the doorbell twice and wait as patiently as possible for a woman in a bathrobe to answer the door. She can grasp by my facial expression, see-through attire, and the Spanish jeers coming from her neighbor's lawn that I am in no mood to answer questions.

She leads me to her kitchen phone and extends her condolences on my start to a very bad Saturday.

A phone call home and an hour later, my grandfather arrives with a pair of jeans, a bra, and dry underwear. Growing up with him as my replacement dad, he spent many years trying to figure out how to fold my underwear on laundry day. Nothing surprised him as far as my undergarments go.

Wanting to avoid the whole wet-t-shirt image, he calls out, "I'll throw your clothes over the fence in 3-2-1." With the lawn dudes gone, I change clothes on the patio in front of Winston's eyes only and call for my granddad to join me so we can devise a plan to get the dog back into the house.

That wet tank comes in handy as we wrap it around his knuckles and he punches through the glass pane by the locked doorknob. My hero.

Never have I been more thankful for air-conditioning, a non-judgmental neighbor, and dry full-bottomed panties.

Lesson Learned: Begin blueprints to design thongs with a cell phone pocket. And unless I plan on being the next slut on *Girls Gone Wild*, no more white tank tops because water is for drinking not for nipples.

Coochie Conundrums

What is it about going to the gynecologist for a "well-woman" check-up that brings on so much anxiety?

I base my appointment on my current weight, which is ridiculous. For some dumb reason, if I am heavier than I was the previous year, I'll call the receptionist to postpone my appointment until I can get off those stubborn ten pounds. It is just plain silly basing my health inspection on a scale.

Then, there's the whole conundrum of pubic hair: To shape or not to shape: that is the question. If you go au naturel, does that make you appear unkempt or like a throw-back to the Jackson Five afro days? Yet, if you show up with some sort of waxed shape, like a heart, does that make you look like a tramp? Invariably, I wake up the morning of my appointment, look down at my overgrowth and ponder what the doctor will think. Should I just toss a little glitter on it and go as a disco ball and give him the highlight of his day? Invariably, I tame it a tad and end up nicking my skin, so I go wearing a tiny square of white toilet paper.

Another problem arises: wet wipes. Wanting to appear as fresh as a daisy for someone who is going to be as up-close and personal as it gets, should I pack some sanitary wipes or will they have some there in the restroom? Better be safe than sorry, so I change to a bigger purse in order to fit the big ol' box without displaying it to the whole world.

Arriving, I encounter the usual annoyance: why is it that I made an appointment months ago for a specific time, yet, when I sign in at the receptionist's desk, there are five other women with the exact same appointment time? Seriously? As I'm handed the information sheet, it often has my personal info … my VERY personal info … attached to it, which is quite fascinating. I try to figure out what codes and abbreviations mean, praying that it doesn't say, "Funk alert!" or "Flabby labia issues." Luckily, nothing too harsh stands out--yet.

Invariably, the waiting room proves to be of interest. There sits me, the one just needing a pap smear, yet I notice the overly-pregnant chick off to the side, which makes me pray the doctor doesn't accidentally break her water, which will cause me to have to wait an additional 45 minutes. Then, there is the loud cell-phone talker who is sharing personal information about an unexpected positive pregnancy test to a room full of apprehensive women. Then, in rushes the jittery girl about 20 years old who demands to see the doctor at "the first available slot" because she has an "emergency situation" … hmm. And, there's me: just sitting in an awkward position trying not to create crotch sweat and repositioning myself as not to scratch the new razor-burn on my nether-regions.

Finally, my name is called. Why is it the nurse always wants to weigh me BEFORE I leave the urine sample? Doesn't she know I drank 40 ounces of liquid while on my drive to the doctor's office in order to try and pee out any water-weight from leftover sodium from the night before? I spot the dreaded, official scale that is positioned in the hallway for anyone to see while passing by. Insisting I use the restroom first, much to the chagrin of the nurse who is in a hurry, I wiggle out every last drop, freshen myself … again … and take off every piece of jewelry, every stray bobby pin, and discard my belt. Voila! I'm ready to be weighed. Mentally, I tell myself to remove 3 pounds from whatever number I see because clothes weigh 2 pounds and my breakfast probably accounts for 1 pound.

What is it about sitting in a freezing examining room with a piece of paper covering my naked body that makes me sweat like an ovulating wild hog in August? Nerves, perhaps. I usually make my husband buy me a nice dinner or at least unload the dishwasher and take out the trash before he is able to see THIS much of me spread-eagled. Yet, I'm PAYING the doctor to do this to me without any sort of romantic notion beforehand? This is madness!

While exposed and waiting for the doctor to come join me, I wonder what it must be like to be his wife. I can't imagine my husband spending eight hours a day looking at women's coochies and mashing around on breasts to feel for lumps and bumps. I contemplate the level of acrobatic tricks the wife must have to perform in order to even turn-on her gyno-husband or the repertoire of kinky clothing she must wear in order to produce any sort of physical reaction out of him. Yet, her man probably comes home grossed out and not wanting to see another female part to save his life or his marriage.

Finally, the doc arrives. Awkward moment … do you shake hands? No, I know where those hands have been. Do you hug him? Possibly. I've hugged hundreds of people who know me on a far less personal basis. Maybe just a smile, a blush, and a "Howdy!"

Are you supposed to carry on a conversation with him while his face is peering at your innards? Do you apologize for forgetting to shave your legs because you were too wrapped up in shaping the stray squiggly hairs? Do you ask, "How's everything hangin' down there?"

When he is finished, why do I feel the desire to dismount off the table like a gymnast, give him a high five, and a little piece of paper that says, "Call me"? There's not a good way to end this awkward rendezvous.

Praying the nurse doesn't call me to come back in because of something weird like a hidden bladder infection or a yeasty situation, I'm thankful this dreaded journey only occurs once a year.

Lesson Learned: Why on earth am I nervous to show my junk to a man who has made it his career to look at the single-most ugly part of a woman's body fifty times per day? Look around the waiting room. Surely, yours can't possibly be the ugliest hoo-ha he has seen, and if it is, put some glitter on it. Everything looks better when it sparkles.

Ancestral 'Roots'

I have a group of girlfriends with whom I have hung out since the 5th grade. Michelle and I live in Houston; Connie and Lauren live in Austin. Meeting up in various towns in Texas, we convene twice a year to do something girly: no husbands, no children. Just the four of us, credit cards, some junk food, and a big enough SUV to haul around all the "treasures" we buy over our weekend outing.

Usually, we shop either at ginormous outlet malls or in tiny towns that have a craft show in the middle of a cow pasture. This time, Michelle, who works for a hoity-toity company that gives her a lot of perks and prizes, had something else in mind. She was given free spa services to an upscale hotel in Houston. According to the gift certificate, we could eat lunch, have drinks, swim in the meditation pool, sit in the Zen sauna, and receive one spa service of our choice. Since it was the summer time, I decided to get a bikini wax.

Sitting nervously in the waiting area sipping on chamomile tea, I was called to the waxing room by a 6'1" blond Swedish bombshell whose nametag read "Hellga" (nope, not a typo). As I was following her back to the room of torture, I couldn't help but think to myself, "This woman has 'Hell' in her name. This can't be good."

Usually, if someone is going to see my coochie, this person really must buy me something with diamond accents or a great Italian handbag first! That's just etiquette, right? Hellga wasn't much for small talk. She jumped right to the subject of what shape I wanted: a heart, my husband's first initial, the Brazilian, an airplane landing strip … I chose "The Hitler," a tiny 'stache with fierce edging.

Now I had double whammied myself. HELLga + Hitler= not a pleasant way to spend the afternoon.

Hellga moved my robe out of the way. Awkward. Then, she proceeded to ask me, "What part of the world are your ancestors from?" I had the suspicion she wasn't trying to get to know me better, but instead, this was a loaded question. I replied, "Scotland." She smirked and said in her Swedish accent, "Hmph. From the looks of it, I'm assuming northern Scotland, where it gets really cold!"

Nice. Now, I'm being insulted by the chick who rips off pubic hair for a living. Okay, fine. She's correct. My people hail from frigid northern mountain regions of Scotland.

Going on, the wax was warm, and honestly, kind of nice. Coming off, the wax was EXCRUCIATING! The ripping wouldn't stop. I was panting, squealing, yelping. I heard a buzzing sound like a doorbell, and Hellga excused herself for a minute. Thank you, God! I had a minute to catch my breath. Hellga returned and scolded, "Miss, if you cannot keep quiet, I will be forced to call security. I was just notified that you are frightening the customers in the waiting area."

GOOD! They SHOULD be frightened! Nice relaxation/ spa gift card, Michelle!

The torment continued. This was almost worse than childbirth! She ripped hair from places that I didn't even know grew hair. When she was FINALLY finished tearing out follicle by follicle, I looked in the mirror and truly couldn't decide if it was called "The Hitler" because it looked like his moustache or because of the pain it inflicted.

Lesson Learned: Screw the idea of being neat-and-tidy "down there". Instead, embrace your ancestral "roots" for what they are and spend your money on boy-shorts bathing suits that don't require a bikini wax and are very much in style. Who wants to resemble Hitler anyway?

Just Because You Can Swallow, Doesn't Mean You Should

When my pediatrician tells me it is time to find a gynecologist because it's awkward prescribing birth control pills to his now-married patient, I sigh and feel very nostalgic. I grow attached to people, so leaving Dr. Phillips after 28 years of care will be difficult. Yes. You read that correctly. I saw my pediatrician until I was in my late twenties. Don't judge.

He gives me a few names of area OB/GYNs he knows are really good. Trusting his judgment, I take the plunge and enter the world of big-girl doctors. For some reason, I think I'll prefer going to a male OB/GYN; I just feel better about a man diggin' around in there, instead of a woman. Most might disagree. I see their point, too. To each her own.

As I run through the list of qualified doctors on the piece of paper Dr. Phillips gave me, I stop at the name "Pinky." I think to myself, "Oh, good! I like the sound of that name. It makes me think he has small fingers, and when getting poked and prodded in areas that don't see the light of day, little phalanges are preferable."

I arrive at the appointment, make sure I am fresh as a daisy, and sit in a sterile room wearing a piece of blue paper as a dress that is provided by the nurse who has just gotten all up in my personal business, simply by weighing me. Ugh. After waiting for a while and not knowing whether to leave my socks on or not, in comes the doctor. What a cutie pie! His name does not do him justice. But his hands are by no means tiny, as I had envisioned from his name, Pinky.

He does his duty and confirms what I suspect. Pregnant! I leave feeling elated, nervous, a little pukish, and although I feel guilty admitting it … a little enamored with him. I've heard it is quite "normal" for a woman to develop a tiny, innocent crush on her obstetrician, much to my husband's chagrin.

At my next scheduled appointment, the doctor discovers my progesterone level is low, so he gives me a prescription to help the viability of the pregnancy. Of course, I go straight to the pharmacy and pick it up. I open the medication, which is a single dose enclosed in a clear piece of hard plastic with a thin sheet of aluminum on top. I pop the pill through the top and audibly gag at merely the sight of it; a hungry hippopotamus on a feeding frenzy wouldn't be able to swallow this thing!

With a huge glass of orange juice, I try for thirty minutes to get it down my throat: my eyes water and my throat makes noises that sounded like I'm possessed by Chewbacca. The pill finally turns into a gelatinous goop, which helps it slide down a bit more easily.

Trying to gain sympathy from the torture I've just experienced, I call my childhood friend, Christine, who happens to be a nurse in the emergency room of the same hospital where Pinky delivers babies. I tell her about my evening of trying to swallow this monstrosity. She gets quiet. She stammers over her words. Then, she just giggles … a lot.

She chuckles out the question, "Please tell me you didn't actually swallow it?"

Annoyed at her tone of hilarity, I retort, "Yes! After thirty minutes, it FINALLY went down!"

She inquires, "Umm … Did you read the directions?"

Second-guessing myself, I reply, "No. Should I have?"

Through bouts of laughter, I hear the terrible truth. "Yes, dork! It's not a pill; it's a suppository!"

Freaking gross.

Spazzing out, I think maybe since he delivers babies, who never arrive during normal working hours, there's a slight chance Dr. Pinky is still at his office. I call. I leave message after message, each one sounding more panicked than the last, crying, "Please help me! I just swallowed a SUPPOSITORY!!!"

At eight o'clock the next morning, his nurse calls me. I recognize the number on caller ID, but all I hear is giggling and little syllables trying to become coherent English. She's finally able to spit out the words, "Kasey, this is Melissa at the doctor's office. Thank you for giving us all a fabulous laugh this morning. We've played your messages over and over for each receptionist and nurse who has come in this morning. Then, the doctors arrived, and we played it again for all of them. We're laughing so hard that we're now crying. We can't figure out how you even swallowed that thing! We're impressed! Don't worry, it won't hurt you or the baby, but it does need to be inserted vaginally in order for your body to properly absorb the progesterone, so I'm calling in a new prescription."

Lesson Learned: No matter how simple a task, read the blasted directions first!

Out of the Mouths of ~~Babes~~ Grandmothers

My grandmother is a wonderful woman. She's my best friend, actually. After my parents divorced and my dad ended up on the FBI's Most Wanted list for white-collar crime, my grandparents moved us in with them, which provided stability, unconditional love, and food in our bellies. Day after day for years, each afternoon when my grandmother picked me and a gaggle of my friends up from school, we'd sit in the recliners in the living room and sip hot tea while talking about our successes, hardships, and funny tales.

I received my storytelling ability from her.

Since she was born a girl, her dad, Virgil, could not give her the suffix Junior, so he named her Billy Virgene. She hated it! Shortening it to Gene felt a little better, even though it is still spelled like a boy. She still had the pesky first name to battle, so on her records, it became the first initial only. Being one of the only female students at the University of Texas, sitting in large auditorium classes full of male college students was horrifying on the first day of each semester when the professor would call roll, "Is B.Virgin here? B. Virgin?" She'd shyly raise her hand with mortification and learned to yell across the rows of giggling stares, "It's Virgene. Just call me Gene."

One of my favorite stories of her growing up is the account of her daddy being the president of the bank in Burkburnett, Texas, in the 1930s. As a fifteen year old, her job was to transport a week's worth of money in the backseat of her car to a larger bank in Dallas a couple of hours away. This area of the Lone Star State is precisely where Bonnie and Clyde were tearing things up. She pleaded, "Please don't make me drive thousands of dollars. Those robbers will hunt me down, shoot me, and toss my body in a field to rot!" My great-grandfather replied, "If Bonnie and Clyde discover you, just help them load the loot in their car, use your manners, and let them go on their way. The money is insured, so no big deal!"

Growing up in rural Texas, she not only developed a flirtatious personality as the banker's daughter during the Great Depression, but she also cultivated a deep southern drawl when she speaks. A LOUD southern drawl, actually. Loud enough to yell across a UT auditorium and loud enough to publicly humiliate me at church during a baby shower.

Everyone adores Gene. She is a founding member of our church who has faithfully attended worship services a couple of times per week for the last fifty years and attended every celebratory party ever given. People invite her to their parties just to hear her funny tales. Therefore, getting to sit anywhere close to her is a sought-after privilege. Since she is my grandmother and best friend, this puts me higher up on the pecking order, so I waddle my pregnant body through the sea of her adoring fans at the church's baby shower for another new mom-to-be. She asks how I am feeling, and I explain that I have just been for my monthly check-up with my obstetrician. It is customary for the doctor to perform a test that confirms I am a carrier-host for a particular kind of strep. Supposedly, this is very common and nothing to worry about. I don't really get strep infections, so I'm surprised to hear this, but apparently, I'm able to pass strep to others. Lovely.

The doctor explains the strep can transfer to my baby while she is in the birth canal and cause blindness. He assures me as long as we give intravenous antibiotics during labor and apply a topical ointment to the baby's eyes when she is delivered, her eyesight will not be impaired from the strep. Cool. No harm, no foul.

Gene knows how to inflect her voice at just the right pitch to build suspense and exactly how to land a punch line. However, she also does this sometimes at awkward moments. For instance, while sitting amongst ladies of the congregation who are praying for the mother-to-be Gene announces in her twangy voice, "Excuse me, but could we also pray for my new great-granddaughter's upcoming birth? Kasey's vagina is infected with a disease, so this baby's gonna be born blind! B.L.I.N.D. Blind!"

A disease? Well, butter my butt and call me a biscuit! I'd hardly call strep a disease!

Hell hath no fury like a woman scorned! Psh. No. Hell hath no fury like a pregnant woman judged!

I give my best southern wave to the crowd of conservative Church of Christ ladies and say, "Thanks for the prayers, y'all." Then, I slink my invisible tail between my strep-infected crotch and wobble outta there as fast as I can.

Lesson Learned: Less is more. Neither grandmothers, nor anyone else for that matter, needs to know the details of what goes on in the birth canal. Some topics are better left untouched … and apparently, so are some vaginas.

Does Size Really Matter?

When I get pregnant with my first child, I am dancing with a professional modern dance company in Houston during the evenings and weekends, while teaching English to ninth graders during the day. You have to wonder how I even find the time to get pregnant.

My dance partner, Emilio, discovers pretty quickly that I'm retaining water ...or fat... or a baby. When we do lifts, my center of gravity feels differently to him. Right away, he suspects something is up. After I'm dropped a few times and start to bleed a little, probably from catapulting from seven feet in the air to a hardwood floor, my doctor gives me two options: 1) continue to dance, or 2) have a baby.

I choose the baby.

I also choose the next several months to eat my way into oblivion. Always having to watch my weight because of crappy genetics and wearing unforgiving leotards on stage, I am very careful about what I eat. Now that I won't be in a shiny, spandex contraption for a while, I become a slave to sugar and obey its every command.

Every day is the same ritual. I get my exercise by going back and forth to the candy machine in the teacher's lounge. Bag after bag of M&Ms are purchased, immediately devoured color by color with the green ones first, and then chased down by a Dr. Pepper. Thus, it isn't long before my weight shoots from 112 pounds to 184. No, you didn't read that incorrectly. And, yes, that is a 72 pound weight gain! Don't judge.

Believe me, I'm reminded of it frequently. Our school janitor comes in my room wiggling booty-licious hips, courtesy of birthing five of her own babies, and says, "Giiiirl, your butt's gettin' big!" Nice. Thanks for the reminder. She waddles past me, opens my desk drawer and dumps out my M&M stash, while promising me she's doing me a favor. The sweet football coach who teaches next door to me feels badly about the janitor denying my craving, so he frequently replenishes my supply.

For some reason, I refuse to believe the 72 pounds I'm gaining are due to the gargantuous amount of empty calories I'm consuming. I tell myself and anyone else who makes judgmental comments to me that I just retain a lot of water; it's no big deal because some pregnant women gain more than others. Right?

Eating feels quite liberating. And hey, I actually have boobs now, so it can't be all that bad!

The baby is late; after all, she is a product of her mother! So, I wake up at the crack of dawn to be induced. The labor goes super fast, and as I'm in between my three … yes, just three … pushes, the baby slithers right out. I raise my head, look at the doctor and ask, "Am I a size 4 again?"

He laughs and retorts, "The last time I was a size 4, I was 8 years old!" Not missing a beat, the very curvy nurse adds, "Ha! When I was 4 years old, I was a size 8!" They both look me over and I see the look sprawled on their faces, meaning, "Honey, it'll take a while. Size 4 is nowhere to be found on that body!"

After they weigh my baby, I disappointedly realize she does not weigh 72 pounds at all, but merely 7 pounds and 6 ounces. Not at all what I was anticipating! I thought she'd at least be 11 pounds, plus 51 pounds of placenta and water, plus 5 pounds for each of my new mommy-boobs.

So, off to the gym I go to burn off each individual M&M, the green ones first.

Lesson Learned: Although size should not matter, let's face it, in the self-image of a new mom, feeling good about your body is right up there with a full night's sleep and an anti-depressant pill. Irreplaceable.

Permanent Scars: Tats Vs. Teenagers

The school where I teach has two groups of kids- an AM group and a PM group. Both are bussed in from their home high school to my campus for specialty classes. In between these two groups, the teachers have an hour and a half break, used for lunch, meetings, lesson planning, and grading. Generally speaking, there are no students in the school during this break just teachers busily working in our classrooms.

At the end of the hallway, I'm minding my own business while bending over rearranging my book shelf. Another English teacher bee-bops into my room, gasps, and exclaims, "You have a tattoo?!?!" Without looking up, I grab the side of my panties, lift them up and out of my pants, and reply, "Not only do I have a tramp stamp, but I'm also sporting a hot pink lace thong, baaaby!"

Hearing a grunt of disgust, we both glance over, and standing in the doorway of my room is my student, Tanner. His face looks like he might dry heave right then and there. He waves his hands frantically in front of his chest, wrinkles his nose, and says, "I just swung by to see if you had any recycled paper you wanted me to take to save you a trip."

Oops.

For the next few weeks, Tanner, who is ordinarily not a shy boy, refuses to make eye contact with me during class. It is apparent he just wants to become invisible in my presence. Usually, any 17-year-old boy would love a tramp stamp and a thong ... just not on his middle-aged, English teacher who has stretch marks surrounding hot pink lace and eggplant-colored ink.

Lesson Learned by Tanner: Don't sneak up on someone in places you don't belong. You might not *want* to know what is going on, which is usually too much information to handle.

Lesson Learned by me: There is never an appropriate time to pull panties out of the sides of pants to show them off. Ever.

Hip, Jazz-Hands, Pose ... and Blush

I love to escape into my little dream world as often as I can; however, since I work nine hours a day as a teacher, then come home to my own two kids, four dogs, a husband, various other furry critters, and a house that needs constant de-cluttering, I rarely get to spend ten minutes to myself.

I know I'll be a better wife and mother if I take some time to decompress by soaking in a hot bath to unwind and read my magazine that is frankly targeted toward 20-somethings on the prowl for a relationship and high fashion, not almost-40-somethings who have major stretch marks and more craters on the back of their thighs than the surface of the moon. Yet, this day, I put aside the bubbles and magazine and press 'play' on my favorite CD, the soundtrack from the movie *Chicago*, and begin to meditate into my alternate persona: Roxy Hart, the sexy antagonist.

The rhythm captures me: the slide of the trombone, the sexiness of the saxophone, the slinky beat of the timpani. I'm inside my own personal play land, a place without baby puke or surprise dog poop I occasionally find in the back of the closet next to the scuffed boots treated with black Sharpie. In my own suburban bathroom, I transform myself into the vivacious vixen.

The blouse is slowly unbuttoned, the skirt slides down with a few rolls of my curves in a rhythmic circle, my hair is released from its much-too-tight ponytail, and each shoe is projectiled with a high kick that would make the Rockettes swoon with jealousy. "Roxy" sure knows how to sashay out of her bra with the wire painfully poking out through the lace and her pregnancy panties (no baby on board … just dang comfy). With this music, I become a hot 1920s flapper, who can wiggle across a black piano, shake her bobbed hair, and swing her tassels into oblivion.

Replaying the song "All That Jazz" over and over again, I perfect my choreographed routine: head sling, blink-blink of the eyelashes, shimmy, shimmy, shimmy, hip pop left, hip pop right, high kick, spin around, jazz hands down over my face (while giving a smoldering look), and pose.

I master it. The volume blasts the hard downbeat of the drums with the slight sound effects escaping my puckered lips, all completely naked because Roxy Hart is the diva of sexy confidence.

This Roxy-of-mine might be smolderingly sexy, but she's not very smart because she forgets to lock the door. On round five of the same song, my husband swings open the door and asks, "Are you okay in here?" during the shimmy, shimmy, shimmy section of my dance.

His eyes widen in disbelief. All that comes out of his mouth is, "It looks like you need a few more minutes to yourself," as he closes the door behind him.

This man has seen me give birth twice, has watched me pump breast milk using a high suction torture device, and has nurtured me through a bad bout of food poisoning, but for some reason, my husband witnessing my Roxy Hart alter-ego is complete mortification for this average ol' gal.

Lesson Learned: Next time, lock the door and use headphones to avoid any suspicion … and just maybe, send the kids to Grandma's house and shimmy for him instead of the mirror … complete with the blond flapper wig and tassels.

Attention Sales Associates: Clean-Up on Aisle Two

With my six weeks of maternity leave almost finished, I am at that awkward stage where I can't squeeze my post-pregnancy hips back into my regular clothes, but I'm too small for my maternity outfits. So, off to Dillard's I go to find some in-between pants to wear to work the following week.

With my new baby snuggled sweetly in her car seat and the car seat popped securely into the stroller, off we go for a shopping adventure together: two girls on a mission.

Wouldn't you know it? The department I need is on the second floor. Peering up with apprehension, I know I need a strategic plan to battle the escalator with a stroller. I've seen other mothers do it all the time; surely, I am just as capable as they are.

Onward!

Getting on the mechanical giant isn't too bad. There's a weird straddling technique that needs some adjustment, but part of the way up, I have it mastered. Looking calm and collected, we begin to approach the top of the ride.

Just thinking I'll roll the stroller right off without complication, I'm not too concerned. What I don't realize is there's a requirement for such a disembarkment: a small but abrupt back wheelie needs to be popped before the roll. Instead, the front wheels get caught on the serrated lip of the exit.

The force of impact causes the car seat to unlatch and hurl forward through the air, while the escalator continues to move and I topple up and over the stroller to splat on the floor, desperately praying I won't cartwheel back down this electric highway to hell.

It feels like I'm living inside a movie with a frame-by-frame slow motion filming trick. Reaching my arms, I desperately try to catch my baby as her car seat topples end-over-end like a football. Running to the rescue, a handsome guy of about twenty-five, hurdles through the air to catch the tumbling car seat. When he grabs it, I envision him spiking it on the ground and doing the 'Iggy Shuffle' in celebration of his touchdown, which thankfully, he doesn't do.

Seeing my baby is still strapped in and relatively safe, I collect my post-maternity body, my diaper bag, my purse that spills all over the ground, and my upside-down stroller. I make my way to my daughter's savior. He hands her to me— the hyperventilating and lacking-good-judgment mother, and scolds, "Ma'am, you really shouldn't have a stroller on an escalator. There's an elevator right around the corner."

Meltdown, I consider using my cell phone to call Child Protective Services to turn myself in for my lack of basic parenting skills. The nice stranger calms me down and escorts me to the elevator, where I exit the store without any new pants and also without my pride, which remains spilled on the second floor at Dillard's.

Lesson Learned: Quit trying to imitate other mothers and follow your gut. They are clearly more agile than me on an electrical moving ground. When in doubt, take the elevator. Or at least come up with a great end-zone dance!

Umm ... I Think You've Seen My Vagina

Have you ever had the experience of knowing without a doubt that you have met someone before, but you simply can't place the exact situation or connection you had with that person? Stupid question. Of course you have.

On a hot and sticky summer night, a group of my girlfriends from church meet up at a ceramic painting place. I won't lie: I'm not overly thrilled about spending money on more crafty junk that I'll eventually need to dust. Plus, I have no clue where I would display a self-painted statue of a fairy sitting daintily on the back of a medieval unicorn; therefore, I choose to bring a bottle of "Tempting Tango" polish for my nails, instead. Hey, I am still technically painting!

The place is shockingly packed! On Thursday nights, Ceramics by Tess closes its doors to children and opens them to the velour-tracksuit-wearing suburban moms, all who range in the 30s-40s age group, for snacks and BYOW(ine). It is amazing how loud this place gets after a couple of hours of worn-out moms collected together with an overabundance of spinach dip and a bottomless carafe of wine, neither of which am I partaking, surprisingly.

So, here I am ... sitting at a long table of giggling confidants, painting my nails and trying to eavesdrop on all conversations occurring simultaneously at our eighteen-foot reserved table, when in walks this lady who catches my attention. I nonchalantly say to my friends at my end of the table, "I know that girl from somewhere ... " It's going to drive me crazy trying to figure out from what area of my life I know her. Did I teach with her at one of my past schools? Did I meet her through a friend and accidentally kiss her younger brother at some swanky party? Did she help a panicked me out of a too-tight outfit with a broken zipper in the dressing room at Macy's?

Ugh! It's driving me crazy! I am also probably tap-dancing on friends' last nerves by harping on the mystery of the unidentifiable chick while they are trying to paint their ceramic turkeys to use as centerpieces on their perfectly decorated Thanksgiving tables.

Finally, it dawns on me! That girl, who frankly needs to eat a bacon cheeseburger, was the delivery room nurse when I gave birth to my first child! Eureka! I figured it out! No one has ever gotten that up-close and personal with me as that delivery room nurse has. And let's face it, those nurses do all the medical work; the doctor, whom I paid $14,000, just catches the baby, and says "Congratulations!" That nurse does all the rest of the goopy work herself!

I feel the maternal need to approach her and her painted gingerbread man Christmas decoration and say, "Hi!" because I sense she and I really bonded during my daughter's birth. My girlfriends stare at me like I have a screw loose, but I'm kind of used to that, and then they question me as to why I feel the need to say anything to this lady whom I barely know. Against their better judgment, I meander my way through metal folding chairs and long tables filled with wine and paint and women who are all too thrilled to be away from their houses full of whining kids.

Arriving next to her, I wait a few seconds for her conversation with her friends at her own big table to draw to a lull, when I spout, "Hi! It's so good to see you again." She narrows her eyebrows and cocks her head to the side. I can tell she is going through a list of scenarios in her head, as I had done previously, as to where on earth she could have met me. To help her out and give her a clue, I remember from six years before that she had a funny sense of humor in the delivery room, so just as the table full of her friends get very quiet, I say out loud, "Umm ... I think you've seen my vagina!"

A little stunned (maybe she needs another glass of wine), she questions, "Excuse me?" Smiling sweetly, I repeat, "I said, 'I think you've seen my vagina.' You might not recognize my face, but maybe you would know my coochie, since you helped pull an eight pound baby out of it."

Her friends' eyeballs look like they are going to spring right out of their skulls like some bad cartoon, while the nurse-lady simply grins. I can see a metaphorical light bulb pop up over her head when she clearly remembers me. She replies through various bouts of giggling, "I wouldn't recognize your vagina because I'm the vet tech who gives your dogs Kirby, Scout, and Sophie their vaccinations at Dr. Clark's vet clinic." (Insert hilarious laughter from her and a few snorts.) She continues, "Dr. Clark is going to crack up when he hears this story tomorrow morning!"

While quickly deciding I need to pull my size 8 foot out of my mouth and slink away with my tail between my ... vagina, I simply reply, "Well ... I guess you've seen my poochies and not my coochie. My mistake. Tell Dr. Clark I said hello."

The next day, I promptly switch to a new vet.

Lesson Learned: Try introducing yourself with a friendly smile and a handshake (if you don't have wet nails at a ceramics place), instead of inserting the 'v' word into the topic of conversation. C'est la vie.

Dang Homonyn:
The Clan Vs. The Klan

My family taught me to be proud of our heritage: yes, first as an American, but secondly, toward my Scottish roots. In a small town called Salado, Texas, there is an annual Scottish festival that is a ton of fun to attend. It's neat to see our clan of extended generations sporting our family plaid of forest green, black, and red and our Scottish crest, while noshing on way-too-buttery short bread cookies and imported Scottish tea.

A Saturday is long enough to listen to blaring bagpipes being marched up and down the town square. A Saturday is also long enough to have my retinas seared by old men with knobby knees wearing kilts that may or may not include underwear underneath. The thought of this is like kryptonite to my brain! However, it is fun being with my people and seeing the parade of fellow Scotsmen who look just like our slew of relatives: a group of red-bearded squatty dudes.

The next night, I meet my two friends, Clark and Celeste, for dinner. Both of these friends are African-American, which doesn't even cross my mind. You see, I believe God created everyone equally. I was taught the song "Jesus Loves the Little Children" from the time I could sit up in a bouncy seat in Sunday School. Now, as a parent, I teach my own children that same song with the very important verse: "Red and yellow, black, brown and white / They are precious in His sight ... " Thankfully, through prayer and teaching, my kids are blind to the various shades of skin color, as well.

However, maybe before I opened my big mouth, I should have thought about the double meanings that may have been construed by my word choice as the dinner conversation led to, "So, what did you do this weekend?" They share their adventures, and then it's my turn to share mine. With their eyes filled with horror, they listened to my story:

"On Saturday, my family and I went out of town to celebrate our heritage. It's called 'The Gathering of the Clans'."

My friends sit up a little straighter in their booth, cock their heads to the side, and ask, "What?"

I repeat, "It's called 'The Gathering of the Clans'."

"The Klans?" they repeat.

"Yes, the Clans."

With an edge to his voice, Clark inquires, "And what do you do when the Klans gather?" I explain, "Our family gets together and meets up with other families of similar ancestry. I fit right in with my glow-in-the-dark white skin and blue eyes."

Celeste's eyes narrow as she grunts, "Uh, huh."

I continue, "We put on our customary uniforms. Then, we have a parade and march down Main Street. Everyone cheers and celebrates our background. When we see our particular Clan raise its banner, we all cheer. It's a ton of fun, and I hope I can continue the tradition with my own children."

The more I talk, the angrier my friends' faces become. Clark just keeps shaking his head with a look of disgust on his face, while Celeste looks like she has a combination of emotions fueling her: sadness, plus a twist of enough fury to knock out Mike Tyson.

For the life of me, I can't figure out why they are so insulted by a bunch of Scottish people wearing plaid and trying to immolate our Riverdance fetish while waving the flag of Scotland. Then, it dawns on me: clan, uniforms, parade, cheering, really white people with blue eyes … Klan!

Lesson Learned: Never assume your audience will hear specific cultural words, like "clan," as in a Scottish family unit, NOT as Ku Klux KLAN! Oy!

Alert: Creeper at the Pool!

Working fifty hours per week outside the home, I experience guilty-mom-syndrome regularly for not getting to do all the stay-at-home mommy activities with my kids. So during the summer, I feel the bizarre need to enroll my children in every fun activity that our community offers to try and make up for all the time I don't spend with them during the school year. Yes, even though my daughter Katy is fifteen months old and will never remember a single thing!

I book up our calendar with a myriad of play dates, which, let's be honest, are glorified mommy-time when the babies are just a year old and can't truly play yet. These maternal survivor excursions give us an excuse to enjoy face-to-face chat time with our girlfriends and make ourselves feel better about ourselves, whether for getting back into our pre-pregnancy jeans before the other moms or for comparing our child's accomplishments with a dose of catty competition like, "Oh, your baby isn't eating solids yet? Well, *mine* is."

So after the play-dates are penciled in on the monthly schedule, I fill the other days of June through August with an explosion of bonding activities to fill the monotonous days of diapers and puke: mommy-and-me gymnastics, mommy-and-me exercise classes, mommy-and-me church activities, mommy-and-me art classes, and finally, mommy-and-me swim classes.

Being that our money is often tight because my husband and I are both teachers and spend a fortune on daycare (stay-at-home moms, insert audible 'gasp' right here), we find a community pool very reasonably priced, only two miles from our house, and even better. It is an indoor pool to help us escape the July sun in Houston, since my red- headed, overly-pale skin tone glows in the dark, so … score, we hit the jackpot of all pools!

Gazing around the vicinity, on our first visit I cringe at the idea of public pools that consist of crotch-infested waters where strangers' funk is all mixed together. Plus, take a look around. Kids are constantly swishing this water around in their mouths and spewing it out, shouting, "Look Mommy! I'm Shamu!"

Yes, this particular pool is full of people who are three hundred-and-twelve years old doing water aerobics, but they section off a tiny portion for the mommy-and-me swim classes. I can only handle being in the same pool water with old men's sagging scrotums for merely an hour, since the chlorine level is at some illegal proportion just from the smell of the natatorium. Don't get me wrong. I'm thankful for the chemicals, since I have zero desire to ever meet the patrons' crotches personally or French kiss them and experience their dentured saliva, so I'm glad to know these chemicals are killing these germs that float about my baby.

Hoisting my post-baby body into a wired, padded, and definitely solid black swim contraption that promises to suck in my tummy and hoist up my boobs, I put my daughter in the cutest darn swimsuit you've ever seen, and properly position her to hide the baby bulge still nestled right below my sad-looking belly button.

Sneaking away from his summer job to catch a peek, my sweet husband displays pure elation on his face and stars twinkle in his eyes when he looks at his chubby-cheeked baby girl with her wet curls. He desperately wants to catch this moment on video, but each time he tries, Katy spots her daddy and is oh-so-done with swimming. She splashes the water and reaches for her daddy. Finally, on the last day of the summer swim lessons, I look up to see my six-foot-eight-inch, 285 pound, shaved-head, goateed husband looking like an incognito mercenary on stake-out, crouching outside the windows in the bushes with his old-school, giant video recorder pressed to the glass. Admittedly, it looks odd, but whatever. He is capturing his baby's swim lesson on camera, so who cares? What could be more innocent than this?

Well, apparently someone does care because the police are called. While helping our daughter learn to float on her back, I look up to see two cops hoisting my husband up from his crouched lion-hunting position. Being that they are outside, I can't hear the conversation, but it doesn't look like it's going smoothly. At this point, my husband and his two friends in uniform have the undivided attention from all of the one hundred faces (and crotches, don't forget) in the water. At first, I honestly think to myself, "My husband is a rational, calm person who is a teacher all day long to junior high boys in a gym playing games like dodge ball. If anyone knows how to deal with conflict resolution, it's my guy!"

Wrong. My sweet, big dude is so personally offended that the cops think he is doing some sort of pervy videoing of babies, mommies, and senior citizens with gout that he lets his mouth fly! It appears from our end of the pool that words are starting to get heated as arms started flapping around like a rabid bat, as he tries to explain he is just trying to record his daughter's last swim lesson. It doesn't look like any conflict resolution is taking place.

Tired of my husband's indignant attitude toward them in the hot, humid, Houston weather, the cops have had enough. Instead of walking him to the parking lot and escorting him off the property, I guess these guys-in-blue want to get a quick blast of air conditioning, so they open the door next to the window from which the videoing occurs and marches him by the elbow through the front of the indoor pool, while we all watch with gaping mouths and disgusted eyes at this "creepy guy" who videos people in a pool… my dear husband.

While refocusing our attention on our floating babies, the mommy next to me says, "Eww. What a FREAK!" Not wanting to be known as the "freak's" wife, I reply in a disgusted tone, "Uhh! Yeah, I know, right?!!" while continuing to float my baby in an anonymous fashion. Okay, so now you're judging me as a horrible wife, right? I work super hard for my money, and since I pay good money for this honestly ridiculous class, I am going to finish it out no matter what! So … together … mommy and daughter finish the last fifteen minutes of our swim class.

As you can imagine, by the time I change my kid out of her wet bathing suit and swim diaper (Do those things actually work? The idea is almost worse than thinking about the strange crotches in the water!) and re-dress her into something quite fabulous and over-the-top for an indoor pool, I waddle my chlorinated, soggy butt out to the parking lot to see a red-faced, infuriated husband, who seems rather embarrassed, but mostly angry with me for not coming to his rescue from the big-bad-police who confiscated his video tape.

Lesson Learned: What did I learn from this? Well, it makes a great dinner party story, so I'm not sure I would change much if I had to do it all over again. I did learn that no matter how many old people and new mommies have to see me try to hoist my tightly wired and padded swimsuited body out of the pool with baby in tow, I should always rescue my ~~Damsel~~ Dude in Distress … no matter if I paid for a danged lesson or not. Creeper husbands should come first!

White Icing Vs. White Lies

Priding myself in being the self-proclaimed Birthday Party Planning Extraordinaire, I decide to take cake-decorating lessons with two of my girlfriends. Anyone can go to a bakery or even a grocery store and order a child's birthday cake, but it takes a Super Mom to design, bake, and decorate a homemade cake (funny thing: whenever I make flippant judgments like this about other moms, it always comes back to bite me in the butt later).

The class starts on a simple level, learning which silver decorating tips do the cool squiggly lines or which ones create the borders around the cake. After practicing for a couple of lessons and learning how to make the perfect icing flower comes the difficult task of baking the actual cake.

I know … that should be the easy part, right? For others, maybe. For me, impossible. I buy all the fancy fabric wrap-around straps to make sure the cake bakes evenly in the oven, avoiding the lake of buttery batter in the middle; I purchase the pans to create super-cute shapes, and the tool to make sure the cake is not lopsided. I even pay for a cute carrying case for all my new props that are sure to make me a culinary success!

Our next homework assignment is to bring in a baked cake. Some cheat, I can tell; they simply go to the grocery store, ask for an undecorated cake and pay for it. Bamboozlers. Others in the class, like the father-daughter duo, the obvious star students, bake the perfect two-layer cake with a filling in the middle. Suck-ups.

I happen to bake my own with the help of Betty Crocker, and transport it like a professional in a newly acquired domed carrying gadget thingy. Proudly unshielding my homemade confection, the teacher gasps with baker's horror, displays a sad frown and remarks, "Oh, no! Your poor cake! You must have had to slam on the brakes on the drive over here. It looks awful! Let me see if I can salvage it."

Feeling the eyes of the other students silently scoffing at my cake and not wanting to embarrass my abilities any further, I sigh, bow my head in defeat and reply, "Yes, this idiot driving in front of me came to a dead stop. It was either save my car or save my cake. I chose the car."

The teacher goes to work with a carving knife and a big dollop of extra icing, while my girlfriend shot me a glare. I was stone-cold busted.

Life Lesson: Pride is not worth telling a lie. I should have claimed that lopsided cake and decorated it with pride. Or better yet, just buy the dang thing at the grocery store, people. You have nothing to prove to the world of birthday cake analysts!

Sex-Mail Slip-Up

Mr. Forest, the principal of the junior high where I started my teaching career, is in charge of making sure I do a good job in the classroom. He is looking forward to upcoming retirement, but what he doesn't bargain for is a naïve but excited beginning teacher named Kasey who will keep him on his toes for the next year.

Frankly, Mr. Forest scares the snot out of me. He walks past me in the hallway and grumbles under his breath, "Little girl, I've got neck ties older than you," in a very Clint Eastwood manner. I do my best to stay out of his hair and under his radar.

Being inexperienced and desperately trying to keep thirty 13 year olds under control while creating an environment worthy of learning, I need a mental escape during my lunch break. Immediately, I conjure my imagination, and decide to plan a date night for my new husband and me.

Although it isn't smart to send personal emails from my work computer, I can't resist. I jiggle my mouse to freshen the computer screen and begin typing the following: "Hey, hottie! I'm hoping tonight you and I can go out to that new Mexican restaurant for dinner and then you could have ME for dessert!"

Within five minutes, my email dings with a new message. I open it and read, "Sounds like a fun night you've planned, but I'll have to check with my wife first."

WHAT is he talking about? I'm baffled.

I read it three times with a bunched up forehead and wrinkled nose. I reply, "Your WIFE is the one who PLANNED the evening, so she'll approve!" Again, my computer dings, and I read, "You do realize you sent this email to your boss, right?"

Lesson Learned: ALWAYS double check the 'To' box on the email before pushing 'Send'. And if you screw that up, just wear red lipstick to rebuild your lost pride, slyly wink at him, and send his wife an apology letter the next day.

You Can Suck on Me Any Time

Hello, my name is Kasey, and I'm addicted to books about vampires. I seriously need a support group, but admitting it is the first step, right?

For some reason, the sexiness of these blood-sucking creatures is all-consuming. I can melt into one of these storylines and escape the dishes, the whiny kids, and the mountain of laundry for hours on end.

Some books are recently released novels while others date back to vampire lore hundreds of years ago. There are stacks of them on the top shelf of my closet where I keep them housed. At least, I did until I noticed they were taking up space where my jeans used to be neatly folded but now are a rumpled mess shoved in a corner. It is time to find a home or a purpose for these books. My husband's use would be to create a large bonfire with them. I, however, think I've discovered my topic for my master's thesis for graduate school: "The Obsession Modern Day Moms Have with the Ideal Vampire in Literature."

Now, I realize not all women like novels about undead men who put women into a hypnotic daze while nipping at their necks with razor-sharp fangs. Instead, I should be one of those moms reading about how to encourage my child's creativity, how to be a better Biblical wife, or how to change the world with a spatula and a Sharpie. However, that's just not me. I want to be wearing a whale-bone corset with my breasts shoved up to my chin and hair tendriled down to my eighteen-inch waist while a 600-year-old man with clammy skin and perfect facial structure nearly sucks the life out of my powdery-white neck.

What is the outcome? Never growing old or weak. No Botox for wrinkles. No leaky bladder when I sneeze or do jumping jacks. No more stretch marks. Very fulfilling sexual escapades where I'm always in control and have abundant cash flow at my disposal. Heck, I may even wear a black satin cape and speak in a thick, sultry accent. Or, I may even become sparkly. After all, what woman doesn't want to glimmer like a diamond? See? A very tempting fairy tale!

I realize the time I spend reading these books into the wee hours of the morning has become an escape from my own reality. Dishes are piling up, laundry sits unfolded, the dogs' toenails are growing unruly, and the kids haven't had a bath in three days because I use the chlorine in the pool as a valid excuse for cleanliness.

Then I find a plastic baggie with a cluster of fresh garlic in my purse with an attached note from my husband, saying, "Attention Vampires: I want my wife back. Please leave her alone!" Ha. Very funny.

When that doesn't curb my reading addiction, Tom greets me at bed time wearing only glow-in-the-dark plastic vampire teeth he'd bought from a coin machine. He stands there, flexes his muscles, bares his fangs, and slurs the words, "Will this do it for ya?" Okay. Point taken. Put down the books and pay attention to the real life, flesh and bone husband who will eventually get a leaky bladder, sagging testicles, and gray hair on his chest. But at least he is mine, happily all mine. Until the day I die.

Life Lesson: Pay attention to what's right in front of you; that's the reality that will last forever!

What Lurks at the Bottom of the Panty Drawer

After losing the baby weight from my second child, I buy some awesome new jeans. No more "mom jeans" for me. You know the kind: light blue, tapered leg, waistband coming up and over your belly button to make your butt look two miles l-o-n-g. So, I purchase a super stylish dark-washed pair with a small, discreet rip in the thigh and the waistline hitting right where my hip bones used to poke out, two babies prior.

I am so excited to be sportin' my post-baby-weight-loss jeans and bod, that I actually don't mind waking up at the crack of dawn on this Friday morning and going into work. The only drawback from these cute jeans is that all of my pretty panties are in the hamper.

Sometimes, sexy undergarments can make you feel one step better in an outfit because you feel like you have a naughty little secret hiding away that only you know about, right, ladies?! Today won't be that day for me.

I am forced to pull out Those Panties lurking at the bottom of the underwear drawer. Face it ... we ALL have Those Panties: the ones with the lace ripped off every few inches from the elastic like some sort of scalloped woodwork on an old house; a couple of holes in the crotch but still enough fabric to be sanitary; and, laundry-defying stains from leaky tampons. I just tell myself thank goodness no one has to witness this degrading pair of underwear, except for me, unless I get into a serious car accident. Oh, horrors!

This new pair of jeans is a welcomed new staple in my new post-baby wardrobe, even with the dilapidated excuse for underwear, because at the high school where I teach, the employees are allowed to wear jeans on Fridays while sporting our red and white spirit shirts to support our school. I am working late on a "Jeans Friday," when most of my teacher friends are draining their second fruity beverage at the local Mexican cantina. I, on the other hand, am rifling through paperwork and dealing with a discipline issue that occurred earlier that day.

Filling out discipline forms is a tricky chore; since the documents can and may be used in court someday (a teacher's worst nightmare!), and since parents will see the discipline form, the choice of words has to be accurate but strong enough to ensure a stern punishment, according to what the offense is.

Usually, at the end of the week, when kids are sick of school and teachers are even sicker of students, the discipline write-up refers to a kid calling a teacher a "bitch," often with an adjective or two inserted before the "b" word. In this case, my discipline form outlines how I had been called a "fat bitch." I take offense to the "fat" part because I have worked too dang hard counting all of those Weight Watchers points and squishing my butt into hot new jeans to be called "fat" by some acne-infested, body-odor-stinkin', fifteen-year-old freshman who is more concerned about mastering the next level of Halo 3 than reading *Romeo and Juliet.* Okay. I do understand his point about trudging through Shakespeare, but still.

I can let the "bitch" slide, but not the "fat."

At five that afternoon, I stroll into the assistant principal's office to ask him a question about the paperwork I need to fill out for this punk kid. Oh, I need to mention that this particular assistant principal is about my age, shy but funny, and relatively cute according to several teachers on our campus.

Actually, the word "shy" might put it mildly. He once hired me to teach summer school for him and casually asked me what I planned to spend the extra money on. I told him that one session of summer school would be enough for me to buy ½ of the boob job I was saving for, so, I'd buy one boob this summer and teach the following summer to pay for the second boob, and I would eventually have a matched set. He turned twelve shades of burgundy as he walked away briskly. Yes, maybe I should read the district policy on sexual harassment more carefully.

Needing his opinion before I leave to go home for the weekend, I walk right in to his office, as he has an open-door policy, but I realize he is on the phone. He looks up and holds up his index finger, meaning to give him one minute before he can talk with me. I whisper, "I'll run to the restroom and come right back." He nods his head, "Okay."

After peeing quickly, wiggling my sassy-fied jeans back into position, and washing my hands, I sashay my way back into the assistant principal's office. As I ask him my questions about the paperwork I'm filling out, I notice he is staring at my crotch. I think it is odd, but I tell myself, "Well, he's a guy. Whatever." It's obvious he *wants* to look up at my face, but his eyes seem to be glued elsewhere. I am used to the creepy idea of men looking at women's boobs when talking to them, but my crotch? Seriously? Whatever. I ask my questions quickly, declare to myself, "What a perv," and go back into my classroom to finish planning my lesson for the next Monday. Oh, the glorious life of a teacher!

I swing by the grocery store to pick up a rotisserie chicken for dinner, get gas in my car, and then I finally arrive at home. I walk past the big mirror in the bathroom, and much to my complete horror, while in the school restroom, I had tucked my spirit shirt INSIDE my panties ... my period panties! Picture it:

fabulous low-rider jeans with stained, over-the- belly-button cotton panties with a big hole ripped in the waistband of the elastic ... and a red spirit shirt nestled inside. Clearly, there is an art form to tucking shirts into low-rise jeans.

And of course, of ALL the things that are still intact on Those Panties, it has to be the elastic! Now, I understand why he couldn't take his eyes off of my crotch! What I originally thought was a pervy expression on his face--eyes wide, jaw falling open--was more a look of disgust.

The assistant principal being shy, I don't know whether to approach him and explain the situation or to just ignore it and lay low. However, I am mortified that he thinks this is the kind of underwear I don on a daily basis. So, in order to redeem my pride in my panty collection, I plan to walk past him with some super-fantastic hot pink lacey panties hanging out, so that he won't think I am the grody girl with the grody panties.

I never go through with it because I am afraid he'd slap me with a sexual harassment lawsuit, especially after the boob job comment.

From then on, whenever I wear those jeans, he looks me up and down, from crotch to belly out of sheer intrigue, just the same as it is difficult to pull your eyes away from a train wreck. Sadly, I'm the train wreck.

Lesson Learned: Life is too short, so throw away those ugly undies, ladies! You never know when the time will come when they will sneak up and bite you in the butt. Or the belly.

Side note: Did you know that according to my urologist whom I see quite often because of reoccurring, lovely urinary tract infections (TMI?) that when autopsies are performed, the doctor can always tell when the dead person was a teacher because the shape of the bladder is oblong, instead of a regular bladder-shape? Isn't that bizarre? However, if you have ever been a teacher or substituted in a classroom, you know that we do not have the privilege of going pee anytime we need to. We usually hold it all day long, which could be the reason fifteen year olds call us the "b" word ... you do get a tad bitchy with a full bladder by the end of the day. I digress ...

Burning Ring of Fire

My cell phone goes off during class. Never a good sign. The only time this happens is when it's the school nurse calling to say my child is sick and needs to be sent home. Lovely. Unlatching the filing cabinet drawer, I dig through my purse and eventually discover my cell phone lurking at the very bottom. Sure enough. The voice on the other end chirps, "Hi, Mrs. Brooks. This is the nurse at Taylor's preschool. He's running a slight temperature. You need to come pick him up now." Well, crap.

Here I am in a brand new city we tried for a year and hate, so I'm stuck in a place with no family and no friends to call to come to my rescue and retrieve my sick kid. It is too late in the school day to call for a substitute, so what can I do with my last class of 32 tenth graders?

The bell rings to dismiss the class. I now have exactly half an hour during my lunch break to run get Taylor, and I guess, hide him under my desk for the last ninety minutes of school.

Principals don't appreciate it when you smuggle your own children on campus. First, it's a liability for the school; second, it's a distraction to the students; and third, you're adding new germs to the already healthy mix of ickiness in the classroom. Whatever. I have no choice.

Sneaking through the parking lot in a strategic manner, we make it to the back door of the campus. I channel my inner *Cagney and Lacey* detective skills and swoop around the corners to check for any administrative staff. The coast is clear.

The Spiderman blankie makes a nice little pallet under my desk where I place a box of markers with some white paper for drawing, a squished granola bar I keep in my purse for emergency situations, and a few books I located in the backseat of my car. Using a stern voice, I explain to my three-year-old that Mommy is at work, so he must keep very quiet under in his "cool tent" and not talk or bother me while I am teaching the class.

The ban includes singing.

What three-year-old kid do you know of who is addicted to Johnny Cash music? This kid! Name a song from this country music singer, and Taylor can belt out every word in perfect twang. Makes a Texas momma proud.

Following my orders of keeping still and quiet, he shakes his head "yes" in agreement, right as the students enter the classroom.

I get thirty-five minutes into my lesson on the non-fiction novel *Night* by Elie Wiesel, a gut-wrenching, personal account of the author surviving the Holocaust in the death camps for seven horrific years. Thankfully, I'm glad my concealed son is too young to understand the section I am reading out loud to my students, which is about the author marching up to an enormous pit of fire where he'll be pushed in to die.

As I am reading and handing several teenage girls a tissue to dry their eyes from emotion, we hear a teeny-tiny voice begin to sing in a Texas drawl, "I fell in to the burning ring of fire." My students freeze. They look back and forth at each other, not knowing if they correctly heard what they think they've heard, but not understanding where this song is coming from in the room. Pause. Silence.

"I went down, down, down, and the flames went higher." Again. Pause. Silence. Thirty-two pairs of confused eyes searched for the source of the little voice.

Hoping the song will end there, I continue reading.

Suddenly, two little hands pop up on top of my desk, waving in tempo to the song that continues, "And it burned, burned, burned, the ring of fire, the ring of fire." My students' eyeballs widen. A sweet little face pops up and in his best Elvis voice, Taylor says, "Thank ya. Thank ya very much!"

Applause erupts. My son hops out from behind the desk, takes a bow, then quietly retreats back under the desk and begins to color with the markers, reinstating his vow of silence.

I make my students promise not to divulge the secret of my hidden treasure because I don't want to get in trouble with my principal or their parents for exposing them to my kid's fever. We continue our lesson, and in my head, I pray that if Taylor begins an encore performance, he will choose a more appropriate song to sing for the subject matter at hand.

Lesson Learned: If a next time happens, dope the kid up with enough Benadryl to knock him out for 90 minutes so he'll remain quiet while in his imaginary tent. You know you've considered it at times, too.

Don't Judge a Book by Its Cover

Realistically, I know that most of my students will not remember or care about the character motivation of Grendel in the epic adventure *Beowulf* or ponder the complex themes in the novel *Lord of the Flies*. However, my long-term goal is to instill a love of reading books for the sake of discovering new information they can relate to their own lives and for mere pleasure.

On the first day of school, one of my former students, whom I had taught his junior year, comes back to see me as a senior. Loving this kid Michael to pieces, I give him an enthusiastic high-five. (I avoid giving frontal hugs to high school boys, for the sake of my 34DDs causing any sort of involuntary hormonal reaction.)

I say, "Hi! How was your summer?" He replies, "Well, that's what I came to tell you about. Remember how last year, you did everything in your power to try and get me to read the assigned books? Remember how I refused, which made my grades suffer? Well, over the summer, guess what happened?"

Shrugging my shoulders, I respond, "What?"

Grinning from ear to ear with pride, Michael answers, "I discovered I love to read! I read book after book after book and couldn't get enough! See- All your hard work eventually paid off, so I wanted to come down and tell you."

Shocked, but pleased to learn I have finally made an impression on him, I inquire, "Really?? What changed?"

"Well, I spent my summer in jail."

Oh, Lordy.

He continues, "There was nothing to do except read books or play dominoes. So, I got really good at both."

For once, I'm speechless, wondering what an appropriate teacher reply should be. Stumped, I just high-five him a second time, and conclude with, "Well, I'm proud of your new love of reading."

Lesson Learned: I guess it's somewhat comforting to know that while educating today's youth, I'm also educating the prison population. Multi-tasking at its finest.

Burned Retinas

My husband Tom is driving to work at 6:30AM and receives a phone call from his mom. Like so many doting parents, she is concerned her daughter-in-law isn't servicing her precious baby boy properly in the bedroom. He tells her that he doesn't feel comfortable talking with her about his sex life and with annoyance hangs up.

Not getting the response she wants from Tom, she comes over to my house to use our computer and begins this incredibly awkward conversation with me:

"I'm worried about my son's sex life." Shocked, I respond, "Umm … Why?" She replies, "Well, last weekend, I kept the kids while y'all went on a date. I was expecting you to go somewhere romantic to eat, but instead, y'all went to a movie and ate at the food court in the mall. That's not romantic at all."

I explain to her that we both wanted to see a particular movie that had nothing to do with kids' cartoons or princesses or a G-rating, so we took this opportunity to see it on our date night. With the way the movie time worked out, we didn't have time to go to a restaurant first, so we just went to the food court. No big deal.

She wrinkles her nose and says, "Well, since your date was not romantic, I hope you at least gave my son hot sex when y'all got back home!"

What the ****?

Surely, I'm being "punked." I just know any moment, Ashton Kutcher will jump out with the hidden video camera and fist-pump me for being a good sport in awkward conversation.

I am not a prude when it comes to talking about sex. In fact, I have entertained many dinner parties and girls' nights with sex-talk; it's educational and quite entertaining. However, sex talk should occur with fellow girlfriends, not with my mother-in-law!

Uncomfortable with the direction this discussion is heading and trying to squelch the topic so my kids, who are watching TV in the next room, won't overhear, I whisper, "Tom is well taken care of," hoping she will drop the subject. Instead, this opens a can of wiggly worms. Wiggly phallic worms.

She beams, "Oh, that's good to hear! I want to give you some tips you can try in the bedroom that I enjoyed when I was married." My eyes about pop out of my skull. Not taking the cue from my bug-eyed expression, she continues to tell me about certain positions she enjoyed, how loudly she moaned, and some adventures I should try that her son will just love. I'll spare you the details … trust me!

When my husband gets home, I say, "Your *mother*..." Rolling his eyes and sighing, he responds, "Oh, no. What happened?" I proceed to fill him in on all the gory details. He audibly gags twice, then cuts me off because he can't stomach any more. His only response is, "I'm so sorry you had to endure that, and I am even more angry that she told you about her kitchen chair trick because (a) that was the kitchen chair I sat in to eat dinner while growing up in her house, and (b) that is MY favorite position, too, so now, we can no longer do that because the vision of HER doing that has burned my retinas."

Sadly, we have never done the chair-thing again.

Lesson Learned: My Aunt Beth has great advice that I agree with wholeheartedly, "The job of a mother-in-law is to wear beige and keep her mouth shut."

Getting Suckered Sucks

I hate when the perfect black turtleneck sweater gets those darn fuzz-balls all over it. I try to pick off as many as possible before I purchase a new one, but when it begins to look frumpy, I head to the store. Three weeks before Christmas is the worst financial time to shop for something other than a gift for someone else, but a black turtleneck is part of my wardrobe staple, as it pairs perfectly with jeans, a skirt, or slacks.

With my toddler in tow, I leave the gym, give Katy a baggie of sliced grapes, and head to Steinmart on our way home to search for the same brand as I'd bought before. Turtlenecks are tricky: too big and they look grandma-ish; too small and every ripple of back-bra-fat is visible. It has to be just the right mix of spandex and cotton, minus the fuzz-balls that appear after too many washings.

Trotting through the parking lot, we arrive at the door. I distinctly remember the man in front of us who is about my age and wearing shorts in December with freshly-shaved legs. I think to myself, "Gosh, I hope he's a swimmer. Otherwise, his sexy-smooth legs are just awkward." He opens the door for us, allows us to walk through, but then walks way too closely for my comfort zone.

Katy and I walk to the women's section to hunt down the perfect turtleneck. Along the way, I find another treasure or two. Why is it that whenever money is tight, like during holiday time or when taxes are due, cute clothes are in abundance? Yet, when I actually have a little extra cash floating in my wallet, not an article of clothing looks appealing whatsoever. The irony of the clothes-god strikes again!

After waiting in line, I write a check for my purchase since I vow not to use my credit card for any more random purchases. Katy yanks my pant-leg and points to the gift-bag section that is only six feet from the cash register. I nod in approval for her to wander over to look at the pretty wrapping supplies. A girl after my own heart. One can never have too many sassy gift sacks.

As I'm handed the receipt from the cashier, the same smooth-legged man puts his hand on my daughter's back and escorts her toward the door. What the (&*^!*&%&^$^%#!?

I grab the sack of new blouses and my turtleneck that will live in my trunk for a week so I don't have to answer the question from my husband, "Is that new?" so I can reply, "Not really." I dart the six feet over to my kid and this creeper. Together, the three of us stand in the doorway as I explain to him in colorful, explicit language that he is to NEVER touch my kid. I scoop up Katy and leave the store with the man behind me saying, "I wasn't going to hurt her," as he slips into the passenger seat of a white Chevy truck that a girl is driving, and they speed off through the parking lot.

Katy and I head next door to Hobby Lobby to purchase an ornament for a Christmas party that weekend. As Katy oohs-and-ahhs over the sparkles and lights on the myriad of Christmas trees, we find the perfect ornament, pay for it, and leave. Holding her hand extra tightly in the parking lot because I'm still freaked out from the Steinmart incident, I feel a tickly texture on my palm. I look down and see a feather.

I stop and inquire, "Katy, where did you get this feather?"

"I found it on the ground next to the ornaments. I think it fell off the pink one."

Wanting to enforce the teachable moment, I say, "Did you pay for the feather with money?"

"No, mommy."

"If you take something from the store without paying for it, that is called stealing. Do you know what happens to people who steal from stores? They go to jail. Do you want to go to jail?"

Okay. I know I might be overreacting a tad, but growing up, my own father spent many years of my life in jail for theft. I don't play when it comes to taking things that don't belong to you without paying for them.

Katy's eyes widen as she shakes her head back and forth.

"What should we do? Maybe we should return it to the store."

Katy nods her head in agreement. So, in we march back to Hobby Lobby and hand the feather to the employee and apologize for taking an item she didn't pay for. As we leave, I pat Katy on the back and tell her I'm proud of her good choice, just as police cars are pulling into the Steinmart/ Hobby Lobby parking lot with blue and red lights flashing.

Katy looks up and asks, "Do you think someone stole something and they are here to take them to jail?"

"Possibly," I respond, not knowing they are actually there to arrest *me.*

After singing "Rudolph the Red Nosed Reindeer" eleven times, we arrive in our driveway and head inside, minus the new clothes. I get Katy all snuggled in for dreams of sugarplums to dance in her head, and the phone rings, "Hello?"

"This is the Harris County Sherriff's Department. Is Kasey Brooks there?"

"This is Kasey Brooks. Umm … Is everything okay?"

"Not for you, ma'am. Were you at Steinmart tonight?"

Gulp. "Yes. Why?"

"I'll ask the questions here. You just answer. Do you own a white Chevy truck?"

"My husband drives that kind of truck." What the heck?

"We need you to drive back to Steinmart. The cashier is waiting until you arrive to identify you as the woman who stole $250 worth of men's dress shirts and ties this evening."

Nervously, I ramble, "There must be some mistake. I bought a black turtleneck and women's blouses. All the blouses were black. I wear too much black, but here I am buying more of it … "

"Ma'am I don't care about the black."

"I have a receipt for what I purchased. I even wrote a check for it. Why would I write a check if I was going to steal other articles of clothing? Wouldn't I just steal my blouses along with the stolen merchandise? See how that doesn't make sense?"

"I didn't say criminals were smart or rational, lady. You have ten minutes to get here."

"But I live eighteen minutes away. I can't be there in ten minutes. Plus, I have a sleeping three year-old whom I'm not going to wake up just because you are claiming to be a sheriff. If you are really a cop, you'd come to my house to arrest me if you think I actually committed a crime."

I hang up.

He calls back.

"You have ten minutes. Starting now."

At this point, I need to talk to my husband. Crap. Now, I'll have to confess I went clothes shopping when I wasn't supposed to spend money on anything unnecessary. But a turtleneck is necessary!

"Tom, so ... umm ... I went shopping tonight. That's beside the point. The main point is the police are waiting for me at the store because they say I stole stuff, which I didn't!"

Tom furls his forehead in confusion, "Someone is setting you up. A real cop would never ask a woman to drive at ten o'clock at night to meet him at a store that has been closed since nine o'clock. This sounds dangerous. You're not going."

"But he said I had to. He said they have me on camera, but I didn't do it. Here," I run out to the trunk to display what I'd bought and the receipt, "are the clothes I bought that I know I probably shouldn't have."

"Let me have the clothes and the receipt. You stay here with Katy, and I'll go to Steinmart. This just doesn't sound right."

Tom leaves in his white Chevy truck. My heart is pounding. I'm not sure why I'm nervous because I did nothing wrong. Feeling nauseated, I try to watch TV. Staring at a not-so-funny sit-com, I'm growing more irritated as the time on the clock keeps ticking by. I've got to get up and go to work in seven hours. I don't have time or energy for this mess.

The phone rings. Finally. "So, I'm in Steinmart with the cashier and two cops. I've watched the surveillance video several times. It clearly shows you walking in the store with some douche-bag looking guy who holds the door open for you and Katy. You say something to him and he nods his head in response. Then, about thirty minutes go by and the video shows the dude putting his hand on Katy's back and walking her toward the exit. Then, you appear and have a conversation with him in the doorway. I can't see what you are saying because your back is toward the camera, but it's definitely you. It shows the three of you walking out together."

(Sigh) I feel like a chump. I got suckered.

Tom continues, "Not only that, but your picture is now printed off and taped next to each cash register in the store." What? My driver's license picture? Are you kidding me? Couldn't they have at least used my Facebook profile picture? Ugh. Now, everyone in town will think I'm not just a thief but a homely thief.

I'm nodding at the conversation, but Tom obviously can't see me, since I'm in my living room and he's inside the security room at Steinmart. I hear the sheriff say, "See. Your wife is having an affair. She's with another man. And that man's not you."

That's when things get ugly. I hear Tom spout off. I hear the cop yell back. This goes on for about thirty seconds when I hear Tom call the cop "Barney Fife." Oh, crap. You just had to go there, didn't you, Tom?

The sheriff calls backup.

Tom is now in "time-out" in the back of a cop car until he settles down. Showing the receipt for the merchandise has not worked. This isn't looking good ... for either of us.

As a back-up cop arrives while Tom is cooling off, the alarms start blaring across the street at Kohl's department store. Tom yells toward the cops, "Hey! Hey! I know you can hear me! Why don't you do your job—let me go and get in your car to chase down the same dude who just ripped off Steinmart. He's clearly on a stealing-spree tonight!"

Tom is right. They receive a message over the walky-talky stating Kohl's has been burglarized. The cops catch the same bald-shinned guy and arrest him.

Around midnight, Tom gets home, frustrated and tired. My phone rings.

"Kasey, this is Deputy Williams. We have the man who robbed Steinmart tonight in custody. We asked him to positively identify the woman who drives the white get-away truck. We showed him the video of the two of you, but he refuses to say if you are the same woman driving the vehicle. Your husband mentioned you are a teacher. So this is a courtesy phone call because I just want to warn you that we do most of our arrests during work hours at the place of the perpetrator's employment. Since you work at a school and there will be children around, you may need to talk to your principal about pulling you from class so we don't place you in handcuffs in front of your students."

"What?! Are you freaking kidding me?" This is so not good. I'm way too cute to go to prison and be forced to hold the pocket of some Amazon-butch-woman whom I'd be forced to let feel my boobies in exchange for safety.

"No, ma'am I'm not kidding. You need to hire a criminal attorney, as well. Don't leave Harris County either or your trouble could multiply. Have a good night."

HAVE A GOOD NIGHT?? I think I might puke. For real.

The high school where I teach just hired a new principal. I've never even met the guy face-to-face, only a brief acknowledgment wave from a distance at a faculty meeting. Here I go, trucking into his office to explain I might get arrested today for theft, of which I am innocent. I know he is thinking, "Yeah, right."

We agree it would be best for my principal to come knock on my classroom door when the police arrive. The plan is to take me down to the front office where I'll be cuffed-and-stuffed so the students won't see it happen, take pictures with their cell phones, and post it all over social media, where my innocence or guilt would no longer even matter. I'd be ruined.

Several hours pass as I teach *Romeo and Juliet* with sweaty palms and a palpitating heart.

Tap. Tap. Tap.

I look up to see my principal's face in the window with his hand waving me to come-on.

"Class, please excuse me. I have to step away for a moment. Someone will be here to stay with you until the bell rings." Tears well up in my eyes. I exit.

Mr. Carol says, "It's time." I gulp and start walking toward his office as I hear a guffaw behind me from two grown men, Mr. Carol and the assistant principal, Mr. Greg. They high-five each other and yell, "Gotcha!" at me.

So. Not. Freaking. Funny.

I smack each one on the arm a couple of times and go back into my classroom to resume teaching the balcony scene where Romeo should be the one arrested for trespassing under Juliet's window.

That afternoon, I find a defense attorney. Buying a turtleneck with our Christmas budget is now the least of my financial worries. I also have to leave the county to go to

Austin for a teaching convention on how to improve the ethics of today's teens. Oh, the irony.

Two long weeks later, the sheriff calls again. He gives no apology for the accusation, the money spent, the energy consumed, and the tears shed for the crime he accused me of, but he does tell me the woman driving the truck has been caught. He also remarks how she has the exact same haircut as me. The chick admits they waited a lengthy amount of time in the Steinmart parking lot looking for a woman who fit her description so they could blame the victim if necessary. I landed straight in their trap of being videoed walking in together, having a brief discussion, and leaving the store together. As we were debating in the doorway, the thief picked up a basket full of neckties and dress shirts and walked out with them and straight to the truck.

I thanked him for the phone call. Prayed a prayer of thanksgiving. Cancelled the attorney. Took a long, peaceful nap to celebrate my freedom knowing I'd never have to cuddle with a cell mate named Big Beulah.

Lesson Learned: Where do I start? Know your surroundings. Be more cautious of strangers. Stick to the dang Christmas budget and forego the turtleneck, which I still can't wear without gagging from bad memories, so it wasn't worth it anyway ... even with 2% Spandex and 98% cashmere.

Wine Me, Dine Me … But Now the Party's Over

Tom and I don't go out on a date often enough. We spend plenty of time together, but it's usually sitting at the kitchen table discussing the best way to explain fifth grade math to our teary-eyed, number-frustrated kid. We also sit on plenty of bleachers at Tae Kwon Do belt testing and soccer tournaments and holler positive comments at our kids' sucky basketball games. We even sit cuddled up on the pew at church. But to actually change out of my yoga pants and go into town for a real date? Rare.

My eighty-seven year old grandmother offers to give my two children painting lessons. She is a gifted artist and Tom and I are desperate for alone time, so we take her up on the offer and instruct our daughter Katy to dial 911 if an emergency occurs.

We scrounge our change drawers for money, check the lint-trap in the dryer, collect half-used gift cards, swipe $30 from our son Taylor's piggy bank (I promise I'll pay it back tomorrow when I run to the bank), and hunt for a two-fer coupon to a Mexican restaurant.

My grandmother gives us permission to stay out extra-long because the watercolor paint takes time to dry, so we decide to go to a movie, too. We're livin' big now!

Before the movie starts, I lean over to Tom and say, "Remember when you were trying to win me over when we were first dating? You took me to the dinner theater. We went on a picnic. Went to the ballet. And my very favorite date was to the art museum to see Degas paintings displayed at a special exhibit. At the end of the date, you surprised me with the Degas book you secretly bought me in the museum's gift shop while I was in awe of the artwork."

Tom nods in remembrance and squeezes my hand sweetly.

I continue, "Now, our dates consist of trying to find the best burrito in town. My, how things have changed."

Expecting to hear something romantic in return or even a promise to do a memorable date the next time we get a babysitter, he whispers in my ear, "When Degas produces a new painting you've never seen before, I'll take you back to see the exhibit."

I reply, "Umm...Degas has been dead for about 150 years."

He winks and says, "Precisely."

Lesson Learned: Although the days of trying to impress each other through idealistic dates are dreamy and fun to remember, there is a lot to be said for being able to go home at the end of the date, put on my ugly stretched-out yoga pants, and unapologetically pass gas from those monotonous dates of burrito eating.

Phallic Fallacy

Part of the reason I think moms have such a difficult time keeping weight off is because of the stress hormone cortisol. According to research, cortisol is the hormone that leads to an accumulation of belly fat.

I blame my jiggle-jaggle on stressful kid-situations, such as Taylor screaming bloody murder in the kitchen. This particular area of the house contains every potential hazard worthy of ending up in the emergency room—knives, can openers, an inferno of flames from combusted popcorn, a blazing oven I sometimes consider locking the kid in during moments of sick fantasy when he's sent another gush of cortisol through my bloodstream to wind up on my hips.

Running to his aid, I see the dog jumping in circles and licking her lips while Taylor stands in his Batman underwear, holding an object in his hand, and frantically yelling, "The dog bit my wienie off!"

Could my sweet schnauzer who adores Taylor be capable of actually circumcising him? Mid-tantrum, he reaches out his hand where rests a wobbly, flesh-colored tip of something unidentifiable and red goop surrounding it.

If there's not a quick lesson on YouTube on how to apply a tourniquet to a bitten-off penis, I'm doomed.

I consider puking. I reconsider this because vomit would add to the list of things I'd have to clean. I contemplate fainting. Passing-out is much less messy, unless I hit my head on the counter on the way down. Maybe I'll just holler, "Best of luck to you!" and run the other direction. This option is the most tempting. No mess to clean up and avoidance are my drugs of choice.

Dang the mom guilt. In mid-trot, I pivot back to return to the scene of the bloody crime. I calm Taylor down enough for him to catch his breath and answer a few triage questions before I have to pack the tip in an Igloo cooler and head to the hospital.

I grab his shoulders, look him in the eye, and demand, "Are you hurt?"

He replies, "It hurts deep in my tummy."

"Are you bleeding?"

"No, that's just ketchup from the snack."

"The dog's snack or your snack? Do we need to go to the hospital?"

Confused, he explains, "The pain in my tummy is because I'm hungry. The dog ate my wienie. My Oscar Meyer wienie, not my ding-dong wienie, but it hurts just the same."

Lesson Learned: Seek clarification in moments of panic to reduce the cortisol effect. I'm convinced skinny moms are the ones who force their kids to sit still on the couch all day with a remote control so no emergencies requiring adrenaline actually occur.

Kids Don't Just Suck Your Boob, They Suck Your Self-Esteem

The title of my maternal role is evolving, and I'm not sure I like it. What was once "mommy,"coupled with a wet, open-mouthed smooch on the cheek and adoration for me gleaming in their eyes, is now just plain ol' "mom," with a side-hug or a cliché fist-bump. Lately, the progression of my label has transformed into "motherrrrr," inflected with an eye roll.

How does this happen in just a decade?

I miss the days of "mommy," when my son's eyes widened with optimistic learning and statements that evoked hilarity, like "Mommy, remember when I was inside your tummy before I was born? I sure miss those days," or even, "Mommy, don't hold that hand. It's my booger-picking hand. Hold the other one, instead." Gross, yes. But at least he appeared concerned about the ick-factor and me not being an integral part of it.

Things are quickly changing.

Morphing into just "mom," I can see the transition of Taylor wanting to still cuddle on my lap and figuring out that boys his age don't necessarily feel comfortable with their mother squishing their cute butt-cheeks and blowing zerberts on their belly. Taylor feigns affection by tooting on my leg or pretends to tell me a sweet secret then burps in an inhuman octave with a wind velocity strong enough to explode my eardrum.

This change becomes apparent when a hot-and-sweaty Taylor bee-bops in the kitchen searching for a cold juice box.

He sees me typing a research paper on the computer and inquires, "Whatcha workin' on?" I reply, "I'm analyzing Freud's Oedipal theory and how it applies to the poem I'm studying." I'm yanked into a headlock that is Taylor's new version of a hug while he asks, "What does that mean?" I explain that Sigmund Freud believes that when boys are toddlers, they are in love with their mothers. As they mature, they end up marrying a woman who looks and acts like their mom because they are secretly attracted to her." Taylor makes an exaggerated gagging sound and responds, "I'd rather puke a million times than marry someone who looks like you."

Thanks.

Lesson Learned: Freud's a freak. And I need a make-over.

I Understand Why Animals Eat Their Offspring

Don't get me wrong—I am proud of my son. I love his tender heart and funny sense of humor, like when he randomly spouts, "I bet it is difficult for British babies to learn to speak with an accent." But I'm just not the type who views my offspring as perfect little entities as some moms think of their kids. We all have quirks. I get that. However, sometimes these children of mine make me want to crawl into a deep hole and change my name to something obscure so it would be difficult for anyone to know that I'm genetically connected to them. Don't judge.

I think I'll rename myself Excelsia Deo during these moments and refuse to answer to the accusatory title "Mom" that traps me into owning them and their humiliating actions.

Second grade was the year Taylor kept me in a constant state of mortification. I'm shocked his teacher even waves a courteous hello to me in Target. Actually, I may misunderstand her greeting when it is really a raised hand to God, praying, "Please, Lord—help my child not to turn out as quirky as Taylor Brooks."

Here is what second grade looks like:

August: Texas has a unique tax-free day right before school begins where sales tax is not applied to clothes, shoes, school supplies, or backpacks. Wanting to scrimp, I equip myself with my battle gear (a credit card and a Diet Coke) to defend my family against the mob of other moms-on-a-mission at the super-sized outlet mall. While we parents make a pit-stop at the kiosk near the food court to discuss the possibility of needing more minutes added to our cell phone plan, Taylor disappears.

It is difficult to look twenty feet in front of us to spot him, given that the mall is packed with shoppers. Trying not to panic, Tom and I split up into different directions to search. Tom heads toward the fast-food area where the free samples of orange-chicken are dispersed to patrons, knowing Taylor has been guilty in the past of collecting several bites by thinking if he changes his walk or puts on sunglasses, the employee won't think he is the same kid seeking repetitive samples.

Nope. No Taylor by the Wok-n-Roll eatery. We check the little train area. The video game store. The arcade.

Panic. Panic. Panic.

Our pace quickens, our imaginations race with horrific scenarios. Twenty minutes pass. No Taylor in sight.

Tom, my daughter Katy, and I meet back up hoping one of us has located Taylor's whereabouts. Deciding to try Bass Pro Shop because our renegade-son loves to look at the fish, we head that direction. As we pass the tween-clothing-place, Justice, I glance at the mannequins to see what clothing will be in style for Katy's 4th grade year. After doing a triple-take, I realize one of the wooden display dolls doesn't look like the rest. Voila! Here is Taylor, posed as a mannequin in the window. Still, staring, and perfectly positioned modeling his clothing ensemble.

Not knowing whether to spank him out of frustration and fear or hug him, I exasperatedly ask, "Where have you been? We've been worried sick!"

Without hesitation, "Showing all the girl shoppers what the cute boys will be wearing this year."

(Face Palm)

September: We begin the school year with Tom completely severing his Achilles's tendon while playing in the coaches versus students basketball game at school. After his surgery to reconnect it, he is placed on medical leave for six long weeks. During this time, Taylor's writing assignment is to tell about his dad's job in honor of career week. Taylor responds, "My dad does nothing all day. He sits with his leg propped up on the coffee table and sits in his underwear watching TV and drinking Coke. He doesn't work, but the government sends him a paycheck anyway." Lovely.

October: I find Taylor sneaking out of my bathroom without making eye contact. His only tasks are to brush his hair and teeth. That's it. Something just doesn't feel right, so I say, "Hold it, buddy. Come back here." I spin him around, look him up-and-down. Nothing appears out of place until I notice a hair hanging out of his shirt. Knowing I shed a lot, I'm not concerned until I yank that one hair and out tumbles a whole cluster of red fuzz like pulling a piece of yarn and watching the entire sweater unravel before my eyes. As the very last of the hair cascades into my hand, I inquire, "What is this?"

He explains, "I come into your bathroom and collect the hair from your brushes and put them under my arms so the girls in class will think I have armpit hair." Eww.

November: The weather isn't bearable in Texas until right before Thanksgiving. At dusk, rolling down the car windows to feel the breeze of 78 degrees feels like a mini-vacation, even when stuck in bumper-to-bumper traffic. Unbeknownst to me, on the way home from Tae Kwon Do, Taylor has slipped out of his little jock strap and is proudly waving it out of the car window for all to see. No wonder the plethora of car passengers that have passed us are waving and laughing. Ugh.

Still enthralled with the strap and cup he has to wear for protection while mock-fighting other classmates, Taylor loves nothing more than to use his male protective gear, which he fondly calls "Thomas," to make knocking sounds against furniture, walls, and even other boys' cups. Nothing thrills him more than to bump it on something and create a joke, "Knock-Knock. Who's there?" Classy.

December: Taylor writes in his school journal, "I wish I had one million dollars so we could buy The Clapper for all of our lights. If I could have The Clapper, I would never have to get off the couch to turn off the lights or turn on the fan. Only rich people can have fancy things like The Clapper." I'm baffled. What part of the theme-song, "Clap on. Clap off. The Clapper," makes Taylor think these people are millionaires?

Thinking she's giving a cool gift, Taylor's great-grandmother gives him The Clapper for Christmas. At night during the holiday break, we can hear him stomping and clapping to the beat of the song "Copa Cabana," while dancing in his Spiderman underwear to the strobe light created by The Clapper. He is thrilled beyond belief—until a month later when the closing of the front door triggers The Clapper to turn on a lamp with his unattended bed sheet sloppily tossed over it. The smell of a burning Star Wars comforter no longer makes Taylor feel fancy but ends up creating some obsessive-compulsive issues toward fire precaution, forcing us to constantly practice drills for escaping a fire. Exhausting.

January: Taylor creates an imaginary friend named Ricky. Using a Sharpie to draw on a pair of eyes and positioning a fake furry mustache, Taylor's hand becomes his alter-ego with a very sassy personality. Ricky is with us at the dinner table where Taylor feeds him bites of food that slip in between his fingers, much to the delight of our Basset Hound. Ricky is with us singing at church. Ricky is with us on the little league basketball court. And even against our threats to put Ricky away in a pocket just for a few quick minutes, Ricky slyly makes his appearance in our family portraits. Forever framed on our wall.

February: I love birthdays. Taylor doesn't feel the same way. Like all the moms in his class, I also want to bring the birthday boy a round of cupcakes so his classmates can celebrate with an overload of high-fructose corn syrup. He begs me not to bring them. Tears are shed. Not wanting to look like a bad mom that I already feel like I am at times, I want to bring the dang cupcakes. I order them, pay thirty bucks, and bring them home so I can take them to school the next day. Repeatedly, he begs to not draw attention to his birthday because he just wants to blend in. I've got news for you, Taylor: kids who have an imaginary friend with a bad 1970s porn mustache don't exactly blend in, dude.

My husband tells me to forget about the cupcakes … all 30 of them that will now beckon me to eat them at night. I send a very grumpy birthday boy to school where his sweet-Pinterest-addicted teacher has made him a giant cupcake with ribbon streamers to be safety-pinned to his shirt for the remainder of the day. She has his classmates circle around him to sing the traditional birthday song … as he melts down into a puddle of tears. Even as a toddler, he hated for this song to be geared at him.

Mrs. Hall gives him a birthday booklet to decorate with a big teddy bear on the front holding balloons and sporting a celebration hat. Taylor takes the black crayon and marks an emphatic "X" over each eye of the bear. He draws a Star Wars light saber that decapitates the bear and draws a wiggly snake slithering toward the paw. Alarmed, his teacher sends him to the counselor's office. The phone call I receive goes like this:

"Hello, Mrs. Brooks. This is Mrs. Wheatly, the counselor at the elementary school. Taylor has been with me for two hours being evaluated because we fear he is depressed and has violent tendencies toward birthdays which aren't normal for a second grader."

Stunned, I reply, "Oh, my. Has something happened?"

She explains the situation with the birthday bear and cupcake corsage, and continues, "Taylor tells me he is allowed to play violent video games at home."

"Umm … Did he tell you this 'violent game' is a *Star Wars* game where all the characters look like Legos? No blood spurts. Just a light saber that pops the squares apart."

Mrs. Wheatly, who doesn't have any children of her own, continues her judgmental berating, "Well, here at our school, we feel a game like this is harmful to the psyche of a young child."

Irreverently, I giggle.

Realizing my snark, she continues, "After spending time discussing his feelings, I feel you don't listen to his true desires, but instead, do what you want to do, not what he wants to do."

Now I'm thoroughly annoyed, "Are you referring to the slew of cupcakes sitting on my kitchen counter right now?"

"Yes, it's about the cupcakes. Taylor tells me he doesn't even like cake or icing. He says he prefers corndogs or Cheetos. Did you consider bringing something your son likes to share with the class?"

"Look, Mrs. Wheatly. I appreciate your concern and the time you have taken with my kid today. However, right now, I'm trying to help him not get his little butt whooped on the playground as he skips around with his imaginary Ricky. I think bringing corndogs is just plain weird and will ensure ostracization from his peers."

"I disagree. You need to focus on Taylor's wishes. I've discussed the possibility of you bringing decorated baggies of Cheetos for each student in the class tomorrow in lieu of cupcakes."

"Oh, really. Not gonna happen. Thanks for your concern. Good day."

... And what was I doing at midnight that night? Decorating dang baggies of Cheetos because that's how I roll.

March: Taylor's assignment for homework is to write about a time he didn't have electricity. Taylor thinks of the perfect example because he recently spent several boring days without power during a typical Texas hurricane. He writes about the decision to draw with pencil and graphing paper next to the light of the window. Yet, this is the journal he turns in to his teacher: "After the storm, we didn't have electricity. I stuck my penile in the penile sharpener so I would know when the electricity came back on. When it did, my penile was sharp." Ouch! Obviously, we need to work on how spelling greatly affects meaning.

April: I ask Taylor about his day at school, "What was your favorite part of today?" He responds, "Well, I had a lot of fun at recess. I pretended I was a flying cow, so I ran around the playground flapping my wings and mooing really loudly." Well, alrighty then. Let's pray he grows out of the flying-cow stage by junior high. And the Ricky stage. And the birthday-corndog-meltdown stage.

May: Taylor's poetry reading for the end-of-the-year celebration is an exciting day for me. My boss nicely lets me leave work for an hour to video my son reading a poem he's written about his family. The other kids read their sweet poems about how much they love ice cream, Disneyworld, and flying kites. The girls love kitties. The boys love superheroes. It's now Taylor's turn. Camera in one hand and flip-cam in the other, I proudly smile as he stands with his written work of art. My quirky boy reads his poem about how his parents hate octopi and how he enjoys kicking wars with his sister. (For the record, neither Tom nor I have EVER mentioned anything about octopi...) Strange.

The other parents awkwardly turn around to look at me with strange expressions. I gingerly smile, look back at Taylor, and give a quiet golf-clap for his effort. His very bizarre effort.

June: Time for summer break. Yahoo! Taylor spends his summer experimenting with various ways to pee in the potty: standing on top of the toilet seat aiming downward, the reverse cowboy, lying down across it with his dingy pointing toward the hole, sideways, front ways, sitting, kneeling, Cirque-du-Soleil style. This can't be normal. No. This is exactly Taylor.

When asked why he can't just stand and pee like all the other boys on the planet, he retorts, "Using the restroom in the same way all the time is boring."

Lesson Learned: Taylor, you are anything but boring. And I wouldn't have you any other way. I'm more than blessed to be your mommy, mom, or motherrrrr.

Got Milk?

After teaching high school for 16 years, nothing much truly shocks me. I have seen and heard it all: stories about drunken weekends, horrific accounts of divorce, gynecological issues, experiences in jail, etc. The list can go on for days.

The longer I teach, the more I see the students' lack of propriety. Girls will raise their hand and I call on them thinking they have a question about *The Great Gatsby*, "So. Umm. Yeah. I'm on the rag. Can I use the restroom?" Oh, gross. Really? What ever happened to, "*May* I please be excused for a moment?" No decorum remains.

I'm not sure I'll ever get used to the decline in society's manners, and this event proves we are going downhill fast. For their Child Development project, two of my students are carrying around very real-life baby dolls that have to be taken care of 24 hours a day, just like real infants. Each doll costs the tax-payers hundreds of dollars, but they are as close to an actual newborn as you can get without actually pushing one out of your own cooch. They pee, demand rocking, giggle, and require regular feedings.

While my students are practicing their writing skills for a dreaded standardized test, I hear a few mechanical whimpers, but I don't think much of it until I hear the boys in class get noisy. Gasp. Giggle. Squirm in seats. Chuckle. "Eww!"

Writing a compound-complex sentence structure cannot possibly be this entertaining. I quiet them down and realize what the problem is: Mandy is "breastfeeding" her baby doll.

Don't get me wrong. I know, I know ... breast is best. However, sitting in an 11th grade English class with hormonally-charged teenage boys, anything that even hints at the idea of a breast is a recipe for disaster. Even the president of La Leche League would at least throw a blanket over this girl for some coverage.

Mandy doesn't have any skin exposed, but she has a contraption attached to her shirt right on her ta-ta. This white, circular, clip-on button with a metal nipple looks like some sort of futuristic pasty a stripper would wear in the year 3013. My student nonchalantly presses the doll's mouth to the button to "feed" it, while the computer chip in the doll's tummy calculates the amount of time it takes to feed a newborn. A timer dings when the baby is "full."

My eyes are the size of golf-balls, "Mandy, no boobs during *The Great Gatsby*, please."

The bottle should have won this go-around. Still, I guess she is being a better "mom" than Crystal, the student sitting next to Mandy, who turns her doll to the "silent" mode for 36 hours straight without ever feeding it because "the crying gets annoying, and I don't want to have to deal with the kid." Seems to me this exercise in her Child Development class is the perfect way to convince all the Crystals in 11th grade they are not remotely close to being ready for a real-life, money-draining, energy-depleting, and time-sucking baby.

I ask Crystal, "Where is your doll? I don't see it."

She states, "Oh, I put my backpack on top of its head to avoid looking at its ugly ol' face."

Lesson Learned: Science needs to create the same little microchip for real-life babies to swallow to allow the option of a 36 hour "silence" mode like they have for the doll. Or perhaps we should be handing out free condoms to all the Crystals. STAT.

Open Mouth, Insert Foot

I have a fabulous friend named Roxy. She is everything that I am not- a rock-hard size 2, long blond hair, super-tan skin, owner of a sports car, collector of $3,000 purses, and PhD after her name. Although we are complete opposites on the hotness scale, Roxy is one of coolest chicks I've ever known who runs with a super fantastic group of non-teacher people whose salaries have about three more digits past what my paycheck will ever have.

Unexpectedly, my two English teacher girlfriends and I receive an email from Roxy asking if we are available to attend a dinner with her at The Junior League of Houston. Lately, my idea of a night on the town is taking my kids to the all-you-can-eat pizza buffet in the strip center at the front of our neighborhood where I can wear yoga pants and a hoodie. I'm absolutely positive that my friend Roxy has never frequented such an eating establishment.

I'm told through the email, "The tickets are $250 a piece, but all of your tickets have been paid for already by my friend. So, put on a sassy black cocktail dress and meet me at seven o'clock next to the open bar." How exciting!

There is no way I'll measure up to Foxy Roxy, but I at least want to look as sassy as my other two friends. Problem: the event takes place before payday. I know I'll have to rummage through my closet to find a dress, instead of running to the store. Ugh.

My daughter stands in the doorway of our closet as I pull out each possible dress and hold it up to display. She wrinkles her nose, shakes her head and says, "Nah" to various choices. Finally, after considering all of the dresses, she remarks, "Well, Mom, it's not great, but this black one'll have to do." Great. Thanks for the ego boost, kid.

The winner by default happens to have been purchased six years prior from Wal-Mart of all places. Don't judge.

Watch out, world … three dressed up moms are on the town! Meeting up to ride together, I am a little shocked to see both the driver and my other friend both drinking out of sippy cups. Toddler sippy cups? At the ages of 35 and 40? They offer me a sippy cup, as well. Ick. Apparently, putting wine in a sippy cup reduces those pesky red wine spills in a car's tan interior.

I offer to be the designated driver.

Trying to appear refined, we sashay our way into The Junior League looking like we own the place and head straight to the open bar. Not being a wine connoisseur, I give mine to my sippy-cup friends and imbibe in a boring ol' glass of iced tea and make my way to the silent auction. $725 for a hand-beaded necklace? Are you freaking kidding me? Clearly, my Wal-Mart dress and I are out of our element.

Roxy spots us and gushes, "Hey, girlies! I'd like to introduce you to the man who bought your tickets. This is my friend, Javier." I am wondering to myself how you thank a complete stranger for randomly buying your $250 dinner ticket. There has to be a catch. Is he expecting this to be like Mardi Gras where he throws me a ticket and I show him my bare boobs? While meeting our sugar daddy of the evening, I quickly ascertain that Javier has zero interest in seeing the chest of anyone with a uterus, thankfully!

Javier shakes our hands politely as we graciously thank him for his generosity, although at this point, we don't say our names, just a simple, "Thanks so much for having us!" He replies, "Roxy told me the three of you are high school English teachers, so I told her to invite y'all to this dinner because you will love the speaker."

I pipe up, "Oh, there's a speaker?"

He explains, "Oh, yes. We are all so excited about hearing this author who has been on the New York Best Seller Book List for three consecutive years! Have you read either of her two books?"

Not having a clue as to who this author is, I respond, "Umm … unless this author writes plots with hot vampire sex in it, I most likely have not read her books."

That comment flies out of my mouth, clearly without being filtered first or seasoned with any sort of decorum. You'd think I'd had something other than iced tea to drink; can you imagine what would escape my mouth if I'd swigged something fermented?

Being a good sport about my verbal faux pas, Javier laughs and says, "Ahh … you must be Kasey!" I blush, seeing my reputation for awkward-situation-syndrome precedes me.

We arrived at a table close to the back of the room which after my vampire sex comment, is probably the best place for me to be anonymous. The server brings out salad as the lights dim and a really intelligent-looking woman takes the stage. My friend leans over to me and whispers, "Hey, that lady is the Mayor of Houston!" Hmm. Maybe this dinner is more important than I originally thought.

The Mayor begins, "Ladies and Gentlemen. Thank you for coming out tonight. It is my privilege to introduce the two people we are here to honor, the first being the president of the national non-profit organization of professional writers who go into public schools to help kids become writers, Mr. Javier

Gonzalez!" Thunderous applause rises from the audience as the very same Javier as the one I'd made a fool of myself in front of approaches the microphone. Again, my friend leans over to me, elbows me, and whispers, "Way to put your foot in your mouth, dork!"

After he so eloquently speaks about how important it is for public schools to use writing as a source of creative expression, several children who are cancer survivors and victims of severe poverty approach the microphone to tell their stories about how this writing program has saved their lives and has given them wings to fly. Now, I really feel like an insensitive moron.

Finally, the famed author, Jeanette Walls, who wrote the memoir *The Glass Castle* and the biographical *Half Broke Horses* gets up to speak. She is inspirational and charismatic, an old soul and a true survivor of life's sticky situations. I'm humbled; I'm touched; I'm moved. My palms turn red from clapping with such exuberance at the conclusion of Jeanette's speech, and I spend the next ten minutes mopping mascara from under my teary eyes.

Javier makes his way back through the crowd as it's beginning to dissipate through the backdoors, gently grabs my hand, smiles, and asks, "Better than vampire sex?" Assume the usual position, Kasey: open mouth, insert foot.

Embarrassed, I apologize vigorously as Javier winks at me and explains, "Oh, giiirl, please. Are you even aware how Roxy and I know each other?"

I sheepishly shake my head, "No."

He continues, "She's my doubles partner in tennis for the gay/lesbian/transvestite league. I wear a fabulous pink tennis outfit and we lie and tell everyone that Roxy is a tranny. Together, we rock the court in style!" Oh, my.

He squeezes my hand, winks, and continues, "It's a true pleasure meeting you, Kasey!" And ... off he goes to entertain the fabulous Jeanette Walls.

Lesson Learned: Without a doubt, know with whom you are speaking and always use a mouth filter. Eating a size-8 foot while wearing a stiletto heel and a little black dress (even one bought at a discount super-center) is a humbling experience.

Pi Is to Be Eaten, Not Calculated!

Math is my nemesis. In school, math and I were never friends. We never invited each other to birthday parties, never sat at the same lunch table, and never passed notes during class. In geometry, I was baffled at the notion of proving a triangle was in fact a triangle, when anyone over the age of 4 can easily look at it and tell it is. Why would I have to prove it using a theory? In word problems, I never understood why we should figure out who is swinging next to a fictitious Laura on the jungle gym if Peter is on the monkey bars and Jose is on the teeter-totter. Who cares?! As long as none of them is bleeding, does it matter who's on the tire swing? You get my point.

In high school, my guidance counselor called me into his office to profess the following, "Kasey, your scores on the last standardized test demonstrate your gifted ability in language arts. Only you and one other student in the entire high school scored this high. However, you are bombing math. So, we'll make you a deal. If you and your mom promise that you will never take another math class at our high school ever again, we've decided to give you the math credit and place you in a gifted English class. That's the deal. Now, make me that promise … "

Buddy, you've got a deal!

This same conversation occurred four years later with my guidance counselor in college. At least I'm consistent.

Now, as the world turns, I'm now the mom with the daughter who likewise hates math. Her 4th grade homework prompt is such: "Parents, please list 10 ways in which you use math in your everyday life." I'm sure most parents in this particular school do use high-level math, since most of the parents of my daughter's classmates seem to be accountants, engineers, and architects; consequently, their answers are presumably awe-inspiring, I'm certain. (Eye roll)

My top ten answers as dutifully recorded for her math teacher are as follows:

1. How many years, weeks, days, and hours are left until retirement, using my multiplication skills?

2. At what velocity and at what rate would I have to exercise to burn off the entire cheesecake I ate while standing in the fridge armed with a fork and menstrual cramps?

3. Speaking of menstrual cramps, it is imperative to divide how many more periods I have to endure before the average age of menopause.

4. What is the safest dose of Benadryl I can administer to my whining kids on a road trip in order to knock them out for 3.5 hours?

5. At what speed do I have to accelerate my oil-deprived engine if I want to arrive on time at karate lessons that are 8 miles away from gymnastics with only 3 minutes to get there?

6. How long can I stretch the $22.60 that is in my checking account until I get paid in five days when I still need to pay for school lunches and enough gasoline to chauffeur my kids to lessons?

7. Now that it's finally payday, what is the cost of these super cute strappy sandals at 30% off of $68?

8. How many fleas on the dog's belly do I have to discover before I'll spend $70 at the vet for new flea repellant?

9. Is it time to start coloring my hair? I divide my age by the amount of gray hair I'm finding in my bangs.

10. What are the map coordinates I'd have to use on the angle of my smile in order to make it appear like I sincerely enjoy a family member's company, when in fact, I don't?

I receive an email from the teacher that just says, "LOL!" Although it may have humiliated my child and is certainly not up to par with the other parents' oh-so-brilliant answers, I earn a 100 that week for my daughter. I think that might have been my first 100 in fourth grade math! Go me!

Lesson Learned: Maybe math is my BFF, after all.

Junk in the Trunk

With the way I treat my car, I'm thankful to teach at a high school that offers Auto Mechanics as an elective. Being a believer in the barter system, I will happily exchange cupcakes for an oil change and tire rotation.

The oil light has been annoyingly dinging at me for over three weeks now, so to rewet my car's whistle, I send an email to the Auto Mechanics teacher to see if he can give me a hook-up that day. No problem. So, I follow the usual drill when I need free work done: I unhook the key from my keychain, promptly break a nail, and give my car key to one of my male students during my fifth period English class, so they can work on my car during sixth period. Then the key will be entrusted to a different student of mine to return the car safely back to my parking spot and deliver my key when he comes to my seventh period class for Senior English. It sounds confusing, but this is how the original plan usually goes down without a hitch.

During sixth period, my classroom phone rings. I try to ignore it, but it's difficult to keep the students' focus during *Canterbury Tales* anyway, much less with the phone ringing. I apologize, run over to my desk, and give the obligatory, "Hello?"

In between bouts of guffaws, the Auto Mechanics teacher, who refers to himself as Big John for reasons I don't want to know because he is only 5'9", says, "Umm, about your car ... my boys need to get inside the trunk to get to the tire-lock tool that is in the little compartment next to your spare tire." I respond with a confused, "Okaaaay," mostly because I have no clue as to where the 'little compartment' exists or even what the heck a 'tire-lock tool' is. You see, I choose what

I drive based on how cute the car is, not by where tools lurk in nifty hiding spots. Big John replies, "Well, the boys opened your trunk, but it had some personal items in it, so I closed the hood and told them they could finish the job tomorrow."

Knowing what a clutter-bug I am and knowing how rarely I even look in my trunk, much less clean it out, I can only guess that it probably is a mess. Without thinking of the students listening to my phone conversation I say, "Sure. Tomorrow's fine. I agree. I have a lot of junk in my trunk." Oh, golly ... I didn't intend for it to come out like that, especially in front of my 28 students who have a difficult time containing the thunderous laughter at my innocent and totally logical comment. Argh.

When I arrive home late that afternoon, knowing my car has a hot date with a fresh can of oil and a tire rotation the next day, I pop the trunk, not expecting to see such utter horror inside!

Before I continue, I need to give you some background to redeem myself, at least in your eyes, since I'll never be able to redeem myself in the eyes of those Auto Mechanic students who sit every day in my classroom learning British Literature from yours truly. Three months prior, my brother had married the love of his life, Elizabeth. The part I was most looking forward to was our girls-night-out for the bridesmaids--nothing too raunchy, just friends dressing up in sassy attire at a swanky restaurant in Houston--and maybe some good, old-fashioned, overly-endowed penile décor gag gifts thrown in for good measure. The fun night on the town came and went, and so did the wedding; however, as I've told you before, I'm quite lazy about cleaning out the trunk of my car. The trunk seems to be the keeper of all leftover junk ... in this case ... an absolutely enormous leftover vibrator, the kind that looks somewhat realistic with veins running through it and that can go from zero to sixty in 1.3 seconds. I try to have decorum, but I thought this would be a funny extra thrown into the bride's gift bag, yet it must have fallen out of the bag, along with some cherry-flavored edible undies. Don't judge.

Upon realizing what my students saw, I freeze. I whimper in shame. I stand in my driveway with my jaw dropped almost to the depth of the hidden compartment where I find that darn little tire tool. I stand there for a good fifteen minutes in shock. After all, I will have these boys sitting in my classroom the next day and for the next eight months, since it is only September!

Horrified by my error, I ask my husband for his advice on how to handle the situation. Stoically, he replies with a stern shake of his head, "Lay low. Don't bring it up. Just act like nothing ever happened." Easy for him to say!

I reluctantly take his advice, and with my head held high like nothing has occurred, I relinquish my car key to my usual set of students the next day. I will say, for the next few weeks, these seventeen-year-old boys are a lot quieter in class and seem to pay much better attention, even though I occasionally catch them giving each other this bizarre little wink with a disgusting little smile or see them give each other a high-five as they enter my classroom.

Lesson Learned: Sexy junk in the trunk belongs on your behind, not in your car.

Out of the Mouths of Babes

Weight gain is my nemesis. Coming from a genetic pool of people who are as wide as they are tall, I constantly battle keeping my weight within the 'normal' range, and I'm often a casualty in this war.

I try very hard to not let my two children witness my tantrums while standing on the instrument of torture, the scale. However, one morning during my meltdown in the bathroom, my son pokes his head around the corner and shares his 7-year-old, brilliant philosophy on weight: "Mom. Throw that scale away. It just makes you angry. Instead, just sit on the toilet seat. If your bottom hangs down off the sides, then don't eat as much. If your bottom doesn't hang down over the potty, then your size is perfect."

Eureka! This idea may help me conquer the enemy: those light-up, red numbers that mock me.

Lesson Learned: Children are often more insightful than adults.

Webster: You're Needed in Room 120

Strangely, some students have difficulty creating pictures in their head while reading a story. They simply read words without any meaning attached to the letters on the paper. One cognitive exercise I enjoy guiding my students through is drawing a picture of what I am reading, which forces them to focus on the words and attach visual imagery to the story.

One piece of literature I do this activity with is Homer's epic poem *The Odyssey*. In this story, there is a ginormous female monster named Scylla who is camouflaged to resemble the rocks of a mountainside. When boats full of warriors float past her, Scylla's six heads reach out and devour the men with her three rows of shark teeth. This ferocious sea devil also has a cat's tail in the back and four ravenous dog heads attached to her belly, along with twelve tentacles, much like the body of an octopus.

As I am reading the story of Scylla's treacherous body and skill for slaughter, the students silently draw their pictures. At the end of the chapter, the kids finish their masterpieces and tape their drawings to the chalkboard for the class to see what everyone envisioned as I read. The class enjoys the gallery of art, commenting on cool effects of each different picture.

Until we get to the last one hanging on the end. Our heads cock to the side, some eyebrows raise, and I audibly gasp as we all realize that in Matthew's picture, Scylla does not have twelve waving tentacles, but instead, has twelve wavy-haired testicles.

Now, if that doesn't put some imagery in a reader's head, I don't know what else would!

Lesson Learned: Never assume kids understand vocabulary. Always clarify word meaning because if a fifteen-year-old boy doesn't know a word, instead of looking it up or asking for clarification, he will always draw the phallic version. Always.

Who's the A**hole Now?

Something I absolutely cannot tolerate in my classroom is a student bullying another kid. It's unacceptable. A classroom should be an environment where students feel both emotionally and physically safe.

When this safety is breached, I have to take immediate action, yet it's a frustrating experience to have to fill out a discipline form. I have to stop what I'm doing, compose the paperwork, look up the student's ID number, walk ¼ of a mile to the principal's office at the other end of the school during the hall break, call the parent, listen to the parent gripe me out, then use my time to stay after school with the angry kid the next day for detention. Yeah, loads of fun. The whole process is time-consuming and annoying, yet necessary. It's more punishment for the teacher than for the guilty kid.

When I hear Sergio call David an "asshole," I have to step in. Yes, I completely agree with Sergio: David is an asshole! David also needs a good butt-whooping, but my classroom is not the place to handle such frustrations.

In a hurry, I grab a discipline form and fill it out. Being my usual hurried self, I scribble quickly:

Name of Student: Kasey Brooks

ID number: KB975231

Date: October 3, 1998

Offense: Called David an "asshole" during class.

Notice that nowhere on that form is the offender's name mentioned. I have in fact not written-up Sergio, but instead, have accused myself! My true feelings about this kid must have psychologically and inadvertently taken over during the rush.

After second period class, I walk the form down to the principal's office and stick it in his mailbox outside of his door. Not thinking anything else about the issue, I go my merry way to lunch.

Locking my door with my sandwich and Diet Coke in hand, I turn and bump right into Mr. Forest. In his gruff, Marine Corps voice, he states, "Young lady. It is not appropriate to call any of your students an asshole. Are you begging to get fired?" Then, he briskly walks away.

I'm stunned. Reminding myself to breathe, I am not really sure what has just happened, but I know there must have been some sort of communication glitch. I would never call a student such a word, because frankly, that particular word grosses me out.

I swing by the workroom to pick up my copies for the next day. As I open the door, the paperwork I'd filled out has been photocopied and displayed in twenty different places around the room: "Kasey Brooks called David an asshole." I don't know whether to laugh or cry.

I then enter the teachers' lounge to go eat lunch and see another twenty copies of my paperwork taped to the walls, the fridge, the microwave, and the cabinets. Ha. Joke's on me. That tough Mr. Forrest is indeed a prankster who induces multiple guffaws from the other teachers, and me, throughout the day.

Lessons Learned: 1) As the old cliché goes not judging a book by its cover is so true. The tough, gruff ones are usually the marshmallows with a great sense of humor! 2) Slow down and proof read first!

"Hi-Ya!" ... "Hi-Oww!"

"Mom, pleeease let me show you what I learned in my Tae Kwon Do class yesterday," Taylor begs.

"Tay, I've got three loads of laundry to fold, groceries to buy, and 157 tests to grade before tomorrow," I scowl.

"But it'll just take two quick seconds." Yep, Taylor wins. I comply. The mom guilt and his toothless grin beat out my many chores.

Without blinking twice, my seven-year-old son grabs my wrists, twists them up and over the back of his shoulder, and pulls my weight on top of his back. I'm completely immobilized. Yep, he isn't kidding—with just two quick seconds and a loud, "Hi-Ya!" the move is executed.

As he throws my weight off balance and uses his back leg for leverage, I hear a muffled double-pop and immediately feel a sharp pain in my left foot.

I holler. He releases his grip. We both look down and scream.

The bone in the second joint of my toe has broken at a ninety-degree angle going toward the left, while the top joint has broken in a ninety-degree angle going to the right. If I had been on *Sesame Street*, they could have used my toe to teach the letter 'Z'.

I yell for my husband, gasping, "My toe is horribly broken!"

He yells back, "No, I'm sure it's just ... " Then he walks in the room. "Oh, no! That looks horrible!" Yeah, no crap, Colombo.

Breaking into a cold sweat, I pant, "Tom, you handle broken bones all the time while coaching. Just push it back into place and tape it to the toe next to it." He assures me this kind of bone situation is way outside of his expertise. I need a doctor ... on a Sunday afternoon. Before I can resist his suggestion, I pass out on the hard, tile floor.

I wake up to my son pacing while repeatedly saying, "I'm so sorry, Mommy!" and Tom wiggling off my sloppin'-around-the-house clothes to replace them with shorts and a t-shirt. I know he has won—off to the emergency room we go.

Seriously, an emergency room for a dang broken toe? I feel like a hypochondriac moron, looking at real emergencies whizzing past me.

The doctor arrives, looks at it, and winces--which isn't exactly comforting. An hour later, $250 out of pocket, and an ugly orthopedic shoe on my foot, I'm heading home for a six week recovery of a life without stilettos.

At times while hobbling around the house, I swear I can hear tiny crying sounds coming from my fabulous wedges and platforms trapped in the closet, mourning not being displayed on my feet in public. These whimpers become deafening and my fashion pride deflates as I limp along with one orthopedic shoe on the left foot and one flip-flop on the right.

Obviously, my son's Tae Kwon Do lessons are paying off because the kid can definitely defend himself and kick some ~~butt~~ toe in the process.

Lesson Learned: Do not underestimate the power of a 7-year-old boy who loves martial arts. It might also be wise to set aside an extra $250 in the bottom of a coffee can for unexpected emergency runs, such as this.

The Butt of the Joke

There is nothing worse than crotch sweat.

Surviving the summers in Houston is neither for the weak nor the moist. Nothing is less attractive than walking around with trails of butt sweat soaking through the back of my shorts for bystanders to admire. Therefore, I've decided that the only way to fight against this perpetual July nemesis is to wear sundresses every day, which creates a cross-flow of air, allowing as much ventilation as possible in Hell-degree temperatures with 100% humidity.

Sundresses can also be dressed up or down with colorful flip-flops during the day and sassy espadrilles at night. With their versatility and comfort, they can be worn to the movies, out to dinner, and even to an amusement park (I might have missed my calling as a fashion writer).

I stock up on cute summer dresses just in time for my sister and her family who visit us from Saudi Arabia, as they do every summer, since it reaches 130 degrees in the desert. To them, our 25-degree difference in temperatures is a welcome vacation--go figure! To keep our kids entertained, we, along with her in-laws, plan a road trip to Sea World, which with a traditional Buc-ee's* stop, is only about three hours away.

To avoid my butt looking like I sat in the Splash Zone* all day, I wear my breeziest sundress in preparation for potential sweat issues. We walk for miles, applaud beautiful killer whales and seals that twist and flip out of the water, and wish we were the ones in the wetsuits holding onto the dolphins' tails as they glide through the water ... lots of water ... thousands of gallons of it ... I suddenly have to pee desperately!

Navigating a public restroom should be an Olympic sporting event. For some reason, the gods of the stalls seem to have a vendetta against me, so karma always gives me the door that doesn't lock, the purse hook that isn't there, and the one shred of toilet paper clinging to the roll. I wait in the fifteen-minute line and promise myself that if I don't pee on the floor before a stall opens up, I can treat myself to a frozen lemonade. What appears to my bladder to be the opening of the gates of Heaven, the potty is now vacant, and I think I hear angels singing the hallelujah chorus as I waddle to the porcelain throne.

Of course, it is my usual public restroom situation, except this stall actually has toilet seat covers. Miracles happen! But why is it that once you get one of those flimsy paper covers on the seat, when you try to sit down, it shifts and slides to where you are no longer protected? It's almost more of a frustration than it's worth. With a broken latch on the door, proper sanitation requires me to channel my inner Cirque de Soleil skills to hold the door closed with one foot, while the other leg hovers over the poorly-covered toilet like a shaky UFO. Aww, relief.

I finish up, wash my hands, excuse myself through forty women waiting in line, go to see the swimming seals, order a ten-dollar hamburger and a five-dollar bottle of water, then find my family to sit down and eat. As our whole caravan meanders through the crowds to get a seat at the next show, my sister's father-in-law asks, "What on earth are you wearing?"

I reply, "A sundress. In this heat, it's cooler than shorts."

With a big guffaw, he bellows, "No, why are you wearing a toilet seat cover?"

I lurch my neck around, and to my horror, I have tucked the back of my dress into my thong panties with the toilet seat cover perfectly outlining my bare butt. I must have passed by at least two hundred people on my way to the arena, so there is no way to recover gracefully from this incident. The only thing to do is curse the gods of the restroom stalls, find the nearest trash can to throw away their curse of the toilet seat cover, blush a little, and laugh it off.

Lesson Learned: If you see someone walking around looking like a complete moron, always stop and enlighten this person of her fashion faux pas as politely as possible ... BEFORE she walks out of the restroom!

*Buc-ee's: a chain of gas stations in Texas. Everyone in Texas loves to visit this place because they sell everything from furniture, to gourmet foods, to barn sheds. (Yes, I realize that gourmet foods and gas station is an oxymoron, but trust me on this.) They have the cleanest restrooms on the planet and sell t-shirts with hilarious slogans. If you visit Texas, plan to spend at least an hour enjoying the local Buc-ee's. Neither you nor your bladder will regret it.

*Splash Zone: the row of benches at Sea World or other amusement parks, usually inhabited only by overly-hyper children whose parents want to get rid of them for twenty minutes during the show, where they guarantee you will be totally drenched with water.

I Give Up ... Eat Like a Slob!

What is it about little boys and table manners? The enforcement of polite eating etiquette should be an Olympic event.

For the life of me, I'm convinced I spend my entire meal saying, "Use a fork, not your fingers" or "No burping at the table; please excuse yourself" or "It is not necessary to put your foot on the table!"

It never ends.

One evening, flabbergasted at my seven-year-old passing gas and even more disgusted at my forty-year-old husband snickering under his breath at this act, I shout, "Were you two raised in a barn!?!?"

My son swallows his bite of potato and replies, "Well, Mom, Jesus was raised in a barn, and if it's good enough for Jesus, it's good enough for me."

How do you argue with *that* logic?

I'm guessing the Virgin Mary shared similar head-shaking moments, as well, which is somewhat comforting.

Lesson Learned: As hard as we try, moms can't fix the wily ways of what boys think is hilarious. To my son's future wife: I tried ...

My Genes for My Jeans Suck

Texans take pride in jeans. We become so bonded to them that they become our second skin. Our jeans are bedazzled, tailored, fit-to-perfection, and can equally rock a dance floor, work in the barn, or with the right strand of pearls, transform to appropriate dinner attire at a nice restaurant.

I knew the value of a good pair of jeans even when I was in first grade. My teacher told us to get a piece of paper and a pencil and write a letter to Santa Claus requesting the toys we wanted for Christmas. I didn't give two hoots about that letter until my mom opened the local newspaper and found my wish list printed on page 3:

"Dear Santa, All I want for Christmas is a pair of tight-fittin' jeans."

Clearly, Conway Twitty's songs were heard way too much in my house. And clearly, my attitude was too big for my denim britches. I'm not sure if my mother was proud or mortified at her daughter's request.

With genetics not being in my favor, I yo-yo on and off whatever diet-du-jour I'm on. Finally, I'm able to squeeeeze back into my tight-fittin' jeans. This feat is at the top of my priority list, and the hard work is paying off. To reward myself, I save up enough money for some designer denim and wiggle on the best quality jeans I've ever owned.

Proud of my accomplishments of both saving enough money to buy the darn things and the ability to shove myself back into a size 4, I pop on some great shoes, flashy earrings, and a cute leather belt to accentuate my newly-defined waist. Strutting my stuff as I finish getting ready to leave the house, my six-year-old stares at me up and down, cocks her head to the side, and bursts my ego, "Mom, you think you look good in jeans, but you sooooo don't."

"Oh, really, kid?"

"Yeah, really. Princesses don't wear jeans and you certainly don't look like any princess I've ever seen."

Ouch. True. My tiara has tarnished from six years of wiping her butt, cleaning her waxy ears, and earning money for her survival. A survival I'm not sure will last much longer after her sassy-mouthed attack.

Wanting to ricochet her off the wall, I'm shocked to hear my own mother's voice come out of my mouth, "Sweetheart, there's something called karma. And if it does exist, I hope you have a daughter just like you!"

Lesson Learned: There is no sense in arguing with a kid. They always tell the brutal truth. I clearly am not a size 4, more like a size 8 who had squished into a teeny pair of teenage denim. Listen to the kid, but don't be shocked when karma from your own childhood comes back to bite you in the bedazzled butt.

To Thong or Not to Thong …
That Is the Question

Thanks to the personal narrative, English teachers have read it all. Sadly, we've learned about various kinds of abuse, alcohol use, experimentation with drugs, theft, etc. Although it worries me to read autobiographical stories with my students playing the lead role, it does not usually startle me. So when I assign the essay topic " … And this, I believe" from National Public Radio's popular series, I am floored with Rebecca's essay of what she truly believes is most important in life: wearing thong panties.

At first, I am annoyed. Sometimes, high school students will write about certain topics for shock-value or to test the patience of the teacher. But really, thongs?

My own teachers in school always taught me to start my papers with a definition so the reader is clear on the topic. So, to fulfill this instruction, I'm referring to the word "thong" as underwear, not flip-flops. Because of generational differences, this must be clarified. For example, my brother is also a high school teacher. One day his principal declared on morning announcements, "Thongs are no longer permitted at school due to safety reasons." The girls were baffled and asked, "How will the principal know who is wearing a thong or not and how is it dangerous to other people?" My brother had to explain that flip-flops are also referred to as thongs.

Of course, I also agree that thong underwear can be dangerous. Have you ever been out in public and accidentally witnessed a woman who should have been issued a citation from the cops for accidentally displaying her thong and injuring the retinas of the onlookers when she bends over?

Am I wrong? Either thong can be a dangerous situation, I suppose. Back to the point ...

"Experts" tell teachers that writing in red ink hurts the child's self-esteem, so we are encouraged to use green ink, instead. Whatever. Fine. I comply. So, in *green* ink, I scribble in the margin my usual phrase when things like this occur: "Rebecca, your topic is not appropriate for English class. Please re-write your essay using a different topic and resubmit it to me by Friday."

Something intrigues me because Rebecca is not the type of kid who intentionally seeks negative attention. She is a straight "A" student and a star softball player who cares deeply about her grade point average. So, I decide to keep reading ...

The following is wisdom, according to 17-year-old Rebecca, who states it is imperative that women wear pretty underwear, whether or not the style is a thong, boy short, or full panty. She claims life is too short to wear torn, faded, ugly undergarments. Pretty pink panties are your own private secret. No one knows exactly why you are confident, why you hold your head high, or why you have that extra kick in your step, but you know on the inside. It can also complete an outfit by reducing unsightly panty lines in your skirt. Nice underwear is a double-edged sword in that it can make you feel powerfully strong and sexy all at the same time.

The kinds of literary elements English teachers beg for are all over this essay, including a simile, a metaphor, an allusion to the Mona Lisa, an analogy, and even personification. I am thankful at least one student has taken my lessons to heart!

I've honestly never considered how a thong can be like wearing a Superwoman cape. Rebecca explains that pretty panties are adventurous and empowering, giving women the ability to conquer fears, such as getting up the nerve to ask the cute boy in her speech class to the Sadie Hawkins dance. She explains the boy might never see her thong in person, but it gives her the courage to conquer her fear of rejection.

What do you know? Her theory works. She tells me about her cute dance outfit she bought at the mall and shows me the evidence through a secret little smirk with a twinkle in her eye in the photograph she tapes on the essay.

In the essay even her thong *talks*, "Rebecca, you CAN make an 'A' on your physics test. I've got your back!" Even a pun! Ha! I can honestly say my underwear has never spoken to me; however, we all have that little voice in our head that speaks to us. Maybe Rebecca's voice lives in her lingerie, instead of her brain. Nothing wrong with that, I suppose.

Without a misused comma or a single misspelled word, and more literary elements than I usually require in an essay, Rebecca earns herself a solid "A". The green pen scribbles out my original comment in the margin and below it writes, "You took a chance in your writing, and it worked! Excellent job, Rebecca!"

No, I will not ever encourage a two-page essay about the importance of wearing great underwear, but maybe this seventeen-year-old has some wisdom that we forty-somethings should embrace: a pretty, private secret gives self-confidence and pride. Plus, if you get in a car accident, at least you'll look sexy to that cute emergency room doctor, which is never a bad thing!

Lesson Learned: Although we all prefer different styles of underwear (some don't like the eternal wedgie of a thong while others prefer full-belly coverage), pretty panties *can* make a girl feel put-together. Today, your task is to evaluate your undergarment situation. If your panties have more than 3 holes, one for each leg and one for the tummy, then it's time to go out and purchase a new Superwoman cape disguised as undergarments so you too can conquer the world.

Show-and-Tell Needs a Translator

There's a cemetery about a mile from our house. It is a small lot with newly dug graves, displaying elaborate tombstones, some of which are electric pink crosses. It's definitely a morbidly eye-catching place.

On the way home from school, my six-year-old son, Taylor (the realist), asks if we can go "hang out" at the cemetery for a while. My daughter, Katy (the dreamer), on the other hand, panics fearing a body will come out of the grave and grab us or that we'll accidentally bring home a ghost as a souvenir. Being caught somewhere between a dreamer and a realist myself, I think it is important for kids to know the reality of life and death. They also need a healthy imagination, although more on the lines of forest fairy friends, instead of ghouls grabbing our ankles as we walk past their graves. I guess I see her point.

We pull up to the black wrought-iron gate that clearly displays, NO TRESPASSING on a sign. Now, I am a believer in following rules, but c'mon! It's a cemetery! How are friends and family supposed to visit the remains of their dearly departed if there is NO TRESPASSING allowed? Clearly, this sign doesn't apply to a "normal" family like mine who just wants a glimpse into a local cemetery and its permanent tenants.

Katy keeps saying, "This isn't a smart idea, Mom."

I continue to reply, "Oh, it's fine. Let's go explore!"

She insists, "No way! I'm staying right here in the car."

Raising my shoulders, I say, "Suit yourself. I'll leave the air conditioner running for you. Holler if you need me."

Releasing the latch on the gate, Taylor and I set off to explore the locals. Frankly, it's educational. I get the opportunity to explain the deadly consequences of drinking and driving, we get to figure out how various plots are related in a family tree, and he practices his addition and subtraction by using the birth and death dates to figure out how old the person was when he/she died. What an odd, but yet perfect way, to study for his upcoming math test on Friday!

One particular gravesite that stumps us both is marked for a deceased child who had passed away five years prior. It is festooned with seven very fresh mylar balloons that read, "Get Well Soon!" Taylor and I stand there, cock our heads to the side in confusion and just give each other a bewildered expression. Interesting.

I notice Taylor is walking around with one of the carnations that was left on a nearby grave as a gift to the dead person. We discuss that even though the person is down in the ground and her spirit is elsewhere, it is still considered stealing to take something that doesn't belong to him. He understands and returns the wilted flower. Instead, he wanders over to a bush whose tendrils are growing through the rungs of the iron gate. It has the cutest, tiniest apples (about the size of a large marshmallow) growing from it.

With innocent eyes, he asks, "Would it be stealing from God if I take one of these apples that He grew on the bush?"

"I think it would be okay to take one as a souvenir," I assure him. A "souvenir" from the graveyard? Okay, that's weird, even for me!

Giving in to Katy's hollering from the car window, we return and head home. Without a ghost in tow.

I find out later through the mommy-grapevine that Taylor took the apple to school. Here's how show-and-tell went that day:

Miss Farrell, the most perfect first grade teacher you can possibly imagine—cute, spunky, and caring, says, "Class, Taylor has a souvenir to show us today."

Taylor marches to the front of the class, pulls the little apple from his pocket and announces, "Yesterday, my mom and I picked baby apples that were growing next to a bunch of rotting, dead bodies."

Then he sits down without any further explanation.

Seriously, kid?

Lesson Learned: Didn't Eve get into some sort trouble with picking fruit from the Tree of Knowledge? Remember what happened to that lady, Taylor? She got kicked out of the garden and was made to have childbirth pains. My, how we've come full circle all because of picking that dang apple.

CTRL + ALT + DELETE

You've gotta love those awkward moments that you can never really erase.

But first, I must introduce you to Laverne who is the newest member of our critter family. To give you a visual, she is a 10-year-old Basset Hound, toothless, recovering from heart worms, whip worms, round works, hook worms, and any other sort of worm you can imagine. She also sports 9 swinging boobs. Yes, I realize it should be 8 swinging boobs, but there is a random extra one in the middle that waves proudly to all those who gawk. And true, Laverne is 25 pounds overweight. She is one sassy bitch. Literally.

Due to her fat rolls, Laverne suffers from a grody yeast infection that grows in her pawpits. While walking her on hot days in Texas, I'm scared to death I'll hear a loud pop like that of a biscuit can, and with the combination of her yeast and the 105 degree summer temperature, she'll explode and transform into a croissant right there on the pavement.

It doesn't stop there. Some people say I have too much time on my hands, but to me, it's a creative outlet: I have a Facebook page for Laverne. When I look at her droopy eyes and sashaying rump, something about her speaks to me. No, not in a schizophrenic way, but in an "I'm Mae West, reincarnated" kind of way. She has quite a following of Facebook friends and keeps them entertained by her antics.

Sometimes, it gets confusing as I'm switching back and forth between my own Facebook page and Laverne's page. A few weeks ago, I ignorantly think I am on the dog's page, as I post in celebration, "Hooray! My yeast infection is finally gone!" except horrifically, I post this on my page!

At the time, I don't realize my error and go about my day of running errands and doing household chores. Later that evening, I go back onto Facebook to see if Laverne has received any witty comments under her post.

Much to my dismay, I am the one who gets the funny comments for what my friends think is me getting rid of my yeast infection! Mostly, I receive lots of "T.M.I.!" and "Gross!"

No amount of backpedaling can erase the damage I've done or the icky images I've painted in my friends' minds. Like a dog after a bath, just shake it off.

Lesson Learned: Don't rush while typing on a public website, and always proof read! On second thought, maybe the word "yeast" is never okay to type.

Add This Event to My Daughter's Future Therapy Bill

My daughter is an avid reader. She's also too big for her britches. Dying to move from the world of tea parties and princess costumes, she refers to herself as a "tween."

Tween. That word didn't even exist when I was growing up. Neither did cell phones or the internet, so change can't be all that bad. I guess.

With this in-between stage, she can't seem to read enough books about fictional characters going through puberty. Or as my younger son calls it, "booberty," which makes a whole lot more sense.

As a mom, I struggle with the content of books. How much is too much for an eleven-year-old girl when reading about relationships, praying for your period, or fantasizing about your first kiss? It's a rickety balancing act.

Sitting in my car, waiting for the red light to turn green, Katy asks, "Mom, what are loins?"

Loins? As in what I read in my romance novels? As in, "His hands stroked my loins, desperate for my hot ... " kind of loins? Oh, Lordy. How does a mom begin to explain?

My eyes bulge out like a scared Boston Terrier. My throat suddenly becomes parched. My palms get sweaty as I grip the steering wheel, desperate for the divine rapture to occur so I don't have to explain this word and the context in which it occurs: sex.

Planning my explanation, I stall, "Did you read this word somewhere?"

"Yes."

"Oh. Well, loins are the part of the body that connects your private parts all together. They are the muscles that attach your booty to your thighs and around your hoo-ha. Sometimes when we read the word 'loins,' it's referring to the longing that occurs in that area of the body when a person is ready for sexual activity."

Okay. I think I explained it thoroughly enough. I glance up in the rearview mirror to see Katy's face contort in disgust. Good. I'm not ready for her to think hot, passionate loins are something to long for. I want her to be thoroughly grossed out. At least till she's married.

Out of curiosity, I ask, "Which book are you reading that mentions loins?"

She answers, "I didn't read it in a book. I read it on the grocery store billboard right over there that says, 'Pork loins $3.46 per pound.' Now, I'm really confused and after finding out loins have to do with the 's' word, I can never ever eat pork again. Gross."

Lesson Learned: Before jumping to conclusions, ask the child about the context of a word before creating a visual image she will never be able to scrub out of her brain. On a positive note, Katy is now one step closer to becoming a vegetarian.

Piggy Porn

We live in a barn. It's not an actual barn, but it certainly smells like one toward the end of the week. You see, I strongly believe that having pets teaches kids responsibility and empathy, which in my opinion are severely lacking in today's society. Therefore, when Katy asked for a guinea pig for her eighth birthday, I happily obliged.

Those who know me well have been beaten to death by my soap box of "Adopt! Adopt! Adopt!" when it comes to animals. I am not a believer in going to a pet store when shelters are so full—you've seen the SPCA commercials that bring tears to the eye of anyone with a soul. That being said, I do the horrific, unthinkable deed that goes against my belief of adoption: I give in and go to a dang pet store to buy this baby guinea pig because I don't want to drive 90 minutes in Houston traffic to the guinea pig adoption place. Yes, there is such a place. Trust me. I've researched it. The joy in my daughter's life is now so eloquently named Sprinkles, but he's better known in my head as Freakles.

Katy chooses ~~Freakles~~ Sprinkles after several hours of debating which baby is the prettiest. This is exactly the opposite of what I try to teach my children about beauty being on the inside, not the outside, and judging based on character, not on perfect looks. In other words, I am against pretty animals. I prefer the ones who have two legs and a stub for the third leg that was half-way eaten off by a ferocious beast that is now digesting the fourth leg in its dark lair. I prefer the one with the eyeball hanging out that needs $3,000 worth of surgery to repair it. That's just how I roll in the animal kingdom. I guess I prefer the underdog. It's a weird calling, much to the dismay of my bank account and marriage.

While Katy and I are staring into the guinea pig display at my arch-nemesis, Petco, her Daddy, a non-lover of animals, is at home sweetly assembling a mansion-sized cage right next to my daughter's bed. Katy settles on naming him Sprinkles because his freaky-little-beady eyes are red, like the red sprinkles on a really yummy cupcake. He doesn't look sweet at all. He looks like Satan in a furry suit.

As with most things and most kids, the newness wears off after a couple of months, and after we have all been bitten by this ferocious creature with demonic eyes, I decide that Sprinkles needs a friend to keep him company while we are at work and school. Still feeling guilty from purchasing this little monster from the pet store, I'd decide I will follow my gut and drive the hour and a half to the guinea pig rescue.

In 105-degree weather in Houston, I load up both kids, my mother-in-law, and Sprinkles into my little yellow VW Beetle and begin our trek out north, fully equipped with our drinks from Sonic with the good crunchy ice, the only way to properly take a short road trip.

As we meander our way through the labyrinth of Houston highways, we arrive, not at a facility, but rather at a person's home. Strange. With my legs crossed in order to keep the 44 ounces of Diet Coke imprisoned in my dysfunctional bladder, we pile out of the car with Sprinkles cushioned on a towel.

We walk into the house where a gated community of homeless piggies are playing. These seem to be little bundles of love with long, flowing hair that would make a Pantene hair model envious. In fact, one in particular, named Puddin', shares an uncanny resemblance with Fabio. I'm smitten. Without a doubt, each one of these furry critters can come home with me, and I will be as happy as a clam. Please rest assured that we do not have any pet clams. Yet.

After ooo-ing and ahh-ing over the delectable cuteness of God's tiny creations, we sit Sprinkles in the land of guinea pig-ville to find a new best friend. Low guttural grunts arise from somewhere, but I can't quite figure out what the sound means, as I don't speak fluent Piganese. Possibly the sound is an old-and-much-in-need-of-repair dishwasher? Nope. It's Sprinkles.

The sounds get more intense, more frequent, and more aggressive in pitch. Sprinkles becomes a hot-blooded whirling dervish, circling these other little pigs in a domineering dance exhibition that would rival a peacock in heat. I think surely some of these piggies must be females, and maybe Sprinkles wants to impress them with his Casanova dance from his native New Guinea (or Petco, whatever). Yet, I stand corrected: all the guineas are male in order to help control the guinea pig population. Bob Barker from *The Price is Right* would be so proud of this neutered commune!

Strangely, the dance of love becomes less romantic and more like S&M than what I am personally comfortable seeing. Chunks of hair fly in different directions and squeals of torment echo in the pen as I realize Sprinkles is on top of Crumpet, but backwards, having his way with the other guinea pig's face! Oh, the horrors! A 69 of fur right before my eyes … and more importantly, in front of the eyes of my innocent children … and more dreadfully, in front of my horrified mother-in-law!

The lady who runs the adoptions from her home is just as mortified as I. The speed at which his little pelvis gyrates would have made a hummingbird dizzy. I could not tear my eyes away from this fascinating freak-show, mostly because I've never witnessed something so graphic in all my years upon this planet.

We decide the more submissive guinea pig is probably not enjoying having its fur ripped out by the evil teeth of Sprinkles and his little pecker that's been forcibly jammed in its face over and over. We pull our dominating masochist off of this poor little fellow, who lays there stunned and motionless for way too long.

Maybe Sprinkles just needs to be redirected to a different little guy, so we gently nudge him over to another one, who was sweetly named Puddin' (aka Fabio). Surely, Puddin' and Sprinkles will get along better than he did with Crumpet. Yes, it's fate, I can feel it!

In less than 2.3 seconds, Puddin' is pinned and mounted, again from the opposite direction than he should have been. The low grumble of pleasure turned into shrieks of elation and the gyrations grew more aggressive, when all of a sudden, Sprinkles twitches a little and then relaxes.

Why do I have a mental image of Sprinkles in a Hugh Hefner robe? One with rhinestones, not velvet, in his case, more like Liberace, smoking a Virginia Slim, and leisurely reclining on a leopard print chaise lounge? Back to reality. No. Certainly, I'm imagining what I think will come next (no pun intended). I yank up Sprinkles to relieve Puddin' of this violent scene, when something gooey covers my fingertips.

Have you ever been ejaculated on by a guinea pig? There are no words.

The rescue director is horrified. I don't know whether I should grab Sprinkles and leave a $100 donation toward Puddin's therapy bill or whether to offer to pay for the detangling of his sticky wet fur. Instead, I chicken-out: I thank her for her time, apologize for ~~Sprinkles'~~ Freakles' inexcusable behavior, and get the heck outta Dodge.

There are also no answers that I can possibly give to my kids about what has just transpired, yet we have an hour and a half trip back home. Way too much time for questions.

I find the nearest Dairy Queen and buy everyone ice cream just so our mouths will be too busy eating, instead of having the ability to continue to ask me about the sticky stuff crusted on Sprinkles' belly that now looks like white hardened candle wax.

Have you ever had to soak an angry guinea pig in warm water to loosen up dried semen? It doesn't go well. Eventually, scissors have to make an appearance and after multiple scratches and nips from his teeth, I give up. He chews off the rest of it all by himself, which makes me gag a little.

My only regret is that I didn't pull out a video camera and record the whole ordeal and sell it: S&M Guinea Pig Porn.

Although I haven't researched that genre of porn, I have a strong inclination that I could have made a fortune!

Lesson Learned: Always pack a mini video camera in your purse. You never know when it will come in handy. I could have posted on YouTube and made a fortune from sponsors. And next time, don't forget the wet wipes. Lots of wet wipes.

"Ladies and Gents—Step Right Up to the Freak Show in Cage 3"

On a Sunday afternoon, I'm sitting on the sofa grading research papers as the front door swings open. In marches my son with a gaggle of neighborhood kids. Taylor stops in front of them and announces, "Here she is, guys. Beware. It's realllly freaky!" Their beady little eyes grow wide in anticipation as Taylor holds up his finger, "One at a time, please."

They march closer to me.

I demand, "What are you doing?"

"For fifty cents each, I told my friends they could look at the gross scars all over your belly," he replies cheerfully.

True. My abdomen looks like a road map. It's impossible to tell where one stretch mark begins and one ends. However, he is the exact little creature who came out of me with full Michelin fat rolls who created this post-pregnancy freak show!

Lesson Learned: Throw self-respect out the window and use my budding entrepreneur's monetary proceeds from the viewing of my stretch marks to fund our family vacation! Or a tummy tuck.

Purse-gasm

Remember my insatiable lust for purses that I confessed to you earlier? Fast-forward seven years later from when my first love affair happened with a Brahmin purse. My addiction has grown stronger. I now need two per year. If a twelve-step program would be offered, believe me, I'd be there in attendance every day to rid me of this infatuation.

My credit card is delighted that I've discovered eBay offers brand-spankin'-new, registered-authentic Brahmins. Even though they are still somewhat expensive, just pulling the pictures up on my computer is like internet porn. It excites me, but there's not the same release like touching them in person. Sometimes, it's all that's available, so I have to fire up my laptop and let the lust take over.

The day after Thanksgiving is usually the busiest shopping day of the year. Retail brainwashing is the master at repeatedly putting the phrase into our head "Black Friday." Black. As in nothing could possibly make me happier right now than a big, bulging, black purse.

Black Friday. As in, holy crap, Christmas is almost here, and the last thing I should spend money on is a purse for me when my children will expect stupid ol' Santa to bring them toys they don't need. Oh, but mama needs to get her fix on.

Just to tickle and titillate my desire, I pull up EBay and find the sexiest Brahmin purse ever. Actually, I'll be honest. This one isn't sexy; it's just dang cute. Sometimes a girl needs sexy, and sometimes she needs cute. This one looks like the purse-onified Audrey Hepburn in *Breakfast at Tiffany's*, which is ironically written by Truman Capote who started this whole orgasm cyclone with me.

This purse is sassy, classy, and full of spunk. Sitting at my computer, I can hear my children giggling in the background decorating the Christmas tree. Exhaling with defeat, my conscious gets the best of me, and I close the laptop with a trickle of a tear in my eye.

A week later, I'm at school checking email during my conference period. An email pops up from EBay saying, "Congratulations. You are the highest bidder on a new Brahmin purse." No, I'm not. It's been seven long, lonely days since I've stared at that black, hand-crafted perfection. I click on the link, and there it is, the leather version of Aubrey Hepburn.

Oh, no. Oh, no. OH, NO! Someone hacked my eBay account! I cannot afford this purse right now! Christmas is three weeks away; the HOA is demanding its yearly dues; my Schnauzer has gone without grooming for three months. I definitely did not bid on this purse!

I call my friend Julie to my classroom and whimper, "What do I do? Someone has hacked my account? I can't afford to pay for this purse. eBay has my debit card number stored. This thief could charge my bank account and change the shipping address to her house!" The horror! I wouldn't even get the cute bag!

As we sit staring at the screen, someone outbids this unidentified hacker. Whew. Good. Maybe it's over.

Oops. Maybe not. My hacker rebids. Holy crap on a pogo-stick, I'm screwed.

This event replays itself three more times. Ordinarily, I'm up for multiples ... but not in this situation. Julie and I stare in horror as we watch the bidding war continue. My hacker stops to take a breather on the fourth go-around. No more activity occurs and the other bidder is winning. I click on the shipping address to see where the purse's home destination would be. My address! Nothing had been changed. Odd.

Julie urges, "C'mon, Kasey. It's your address. You just need $5 to win the purse. In the grand scheme of things, $5 more is nothing." I give into temptation. Click.

The third person clicks back. I click again. He clicks back. On and on until I realize there is no way I can afford this purse! What am I thinking? My yearning has taken over my senses. I have to admit defeat to the person pressing "Bid Again."

Although disappointed the Audrey Hepburn won't be snuggled up to my waistline, I feel relief to not have to explain to my kids why Santa left a scrimpy stash this Christmas. The 24th of December arrives. It's Tom's and my turn to open our measly $75-limit gifts to one another. Actually, I love what he got me because it came straight off my wish list: two new vampire novels, dangly rhinestone earrings and some bangle bracelets I'd bought for him to wrap up and give me like they are his idea because I don't like surprises.

Picking the wrapping paper off the floor, Tom says, "Oh, look! Here's a gift you forgot to open." Wait. I got what I wanted. I know I did because I bought most of it or at least pointed at the two books in the bookstore. Ripping off the off-centered bow and paper that does not match my wrapping paper color theme this year, there it is. The Audrey Hepburn!

My eyes bulged in disbelief. "We can't afford this," I squeaked.

Tom explains, "I saved up. It would have been a whole lot cheaper if this idiot would have stopped outbidding me. It was freaking annoying! I started the bidding on your laptop at home because I'd seen over your shoulder that you were drooling over this purse. I placed the bid in the morning before I left for work. When I got to work, I had to create a new eBay profile because all the information was saved on your laptop, and I don't know the password."

I make my way through the obstacle of tissue paper and packing peanuts, jump on his lap, and in between smooches on his lips, say, "I'm the idiot you were bidding against!"

While sitting on his lap, it happens again with Tom's arms around me and the delicious handbag lying on my thighs, ahhhhhhhh. Purse-gasm.

Lesson Learned: Peanut butter and rice for a few weeks won't kill kids. It toughens 'em up. And a 2-week late bill to the Home Owner's Association won't kill me either. It's worth the post-purse-coital glow.

Quite the Charmer

I'm leery about restaurants that have a shopping area attached to the front of the dining area. This is complete manipulation for someone who approaches shopping like a personal challenge. Like I really believe the hostess when she claims there's a 30-minute wait for a family of four to eat pancakes and bacon at 5PM.

Browsing in the candle section, a lady approaches me and calls me by name, so we strike up a conversation. I spend almost the entire waiting time talking about my pet Greyhound, my daughter's gymnastics lessons, and Vacation Bible School at church.

My husband stands by in his usual mute style, slightly eavesdropping but not wanting to admit it. As our name is called by the hostess to head to our table, he remarks, "I can't figure out how you know that lady. At first, I heard you talking about dogs, so I assumed you know her from the Greyhound rescue place. Then, y'all switched topics to gymnastics, so I thought maybe she has a granddaughter in the same class. However, then the topic was switched to VBS at church. Does she go to our church? How do you know her?"

I don't want to admit to it because of my frequent visitations to the place she works, but I'm honest ... and busted. I lower my chin, lift my eyes, smirk and say, "Umm. She is the cashier at James Avery where I go to feed my charm bracelet addiction. I'm there so often, she knows all about my life: dogs, kids, and church."

All he could say is, "So, she's also friends with my Master Card."

146

Lesson Learned: Avoid restaurants with long waits where you may be forced to converse with someone who can give away your sacred shopping secrets. A fast food joint not in your neighborhood might be better. It's quicker, less likely you'll bump into someone you know, and easier on your credit card so you can afford more jewelry.

May I Buy You a ... Car Wash?

My daughter is the kid on the soccer field who does cartwheels on the side of the field while the opposing players score a goal. Even though she decides after the second game that getting pelted in the head with a hard ball really isn't her cup of tea, we insist she finish the season. So, while she pirouettes and picks wildflowers, I sit in my car at the soccer field and read novels I'm currently teaching in my English class, just trying desperately to stay two chapters ahead of my students and praying the kiss-up nerd in the front row hasn't read further in the book than the teacher.

While jotting down notes in the margins of the book, I hear a purring "vroom, vroom" next to me. I look over through my rolled down window at a brand-spanking-new white convertible Corvette with the top down ... and the tanned Australian god positioned in the driver's seat.

I believe in faithful marriages. I'm 100% committed to my sweet husband, but I'm also not blind to other men's obvious hotness. So, when Mr. Australian-Accent-Sexy-Man pulls up beside my car, yep, I notice.

Reminding myself to stay focused on my reading and away from the temptation of checking-out this dude, I plaster my eyes to the book. His engine cuts off, and my son, who is crouched down in the backseat reading *Diary of a Wimpy Kid*, peeks out the window and says to me, "Whoa, cool car!" Taylor slinks back down and keeps reading.

I hear a slight clearing-of-the-throat sound to my right, so I glance over to see the guy smile at me. Not wanting to be rude, I return a quick grin, making sure not to show teeth or do anything sparkly with my eyes. A minute later, I hear him say, "Umm, G'day" in the most glorious accent. Again, not wanting to be rude, I give a quick "hi" and super-glue my eyeballs back to my school work, dependent upon that book to keep me on the straight-and-narrow.

A moment later, I hear two sentences simultaneously: one, horizontally from the backseat and one vertically from the Corvette.

Corvette: "How are you?"

Backseat: "Mom, my tummy hurts."

Like my head is on a swivel stick, with repetition I look from the cutie-pie in the sports car to the kiddo in my backseat. To my horror, Taylor leans his head out of the side window and throws up all over the door of Mr. Hottie's white Corvette.

Lesson Learned: Thankfully, sometimes God throws in something unexpected, like puke, in order to steer you away from temptation. Even when the temptation has a fabulous Australian accent.

They All Look Alike to Me

What is it with guys and trucks?

My husband always says, "See those two trucks? That one is so much cooler than the one next to it. What do you think?"

My response is always the same: "Hmm. They look identical to me."

He huffs in disbelief at my macho-truck-naivete and says, "No way! The black truck has a bigger engine and has more horse power."

This is like speaking Chinese to me. Chevy, Ford, Dodge, Whatever. The trucks are both big and have a rectangular bed for hauling around crap. That's all I care to know about the subject. They all look alike to me.

Leaving the local pizza joint, my husband, two kids, and I walk out to the parking lot with our bellies full and ready to head home in his truck. The three of them go down one aisle of cars and I go down another, thinking I'll meet them in the middle. I arrive at a big, black truck, open the door and hoist my butt three feet up and into the passenger seat. I casually buckle my seatbelt and look over to my left.

Uh, oh. The man in the driver's seat staring at me is definitely not my husband, nor are the two kids sitting in the backseat my offspring. One kid gasps, the other kid giggles, and the man just stares at me in disbelief. I smile sheepishly, bat my eyelashes with southern gentility and say, "Hi! Nice truck!" then literally, get the heck outta Dodge … his Dodge.

Standing outside of this stranger's truck and looking to my right and left to spot the correct destination, I hear my husband call my name from three rows over and ask, "Kasey, what are you doing? That's not my truck!"

Slightly embarrassed and noticing the stranger's wife is giving me the evil-eye through the glass of the "To Go" line inside the restaurant, I give a sincere smile and a gentle wave, then say to my husband, "Don't just stand there and gawk at me. Hit it!"

Lesson Learned: Even though I couldn't care less about the make and model of trucks, I should at least try to memorize the truck that we pay $361 for each month. An antenna ball, possibly?

Shove That Cookie Where the Sun Don't Shine!

Fundraisers, schmundraisers. I'm so sick of selling random crap to earn money for my kids' activities and schools. Do we really need another tub of cookie dough or a magazine subscription? A clear and resounding no! I'd rather just write a check as a donation and be done with it instead of pimping my kid out to pedal the pricey products all over the neighborhood.

But who isn't a sucker for Girl Scout cookies? Those Thin Mints that are so mouth-wateringly pop-able for a glorious thirty calories. Those Caramel D'Lites, that after the third box prove to not be so lite on the hips, beckon me from their little hidey-hole in the pantry, "Come indulge in my coconutty deliciousness!" I oblige. Repeatedly.

I've resigned myself to defeat. I no longer give a flip if my kid sells the most rolls of Christmas wrapping paper in order to win a key chain or whether I earn extra bling in my mommy-crown for selling 583 boxes of Peanut Butter Patties.

Peanut Freaking Butter Patties.

The bane of my existence.

Yet each year, I'm suckered in.

After cleaning out my trunk, I drive my tired butt all the way to pick up load after load of cookies. Tucking the order form securely inside the container, I squish my little Girl Scout in the front seat where I pray we don't get in a fender-bender that would cause the airbag to decapitate her, but what choice do I have since the backseat and trunk are filled to the ceiling with boxes of sugary confections?

Unbeknownst to me, Katy takes the order form out to play with it. Play with it? What in the world does one play with an order form? Somewhere between the facility and our house, she loses it. We search for over a week for that stupid thing. I retrace our steps. I drive back and forth looking for a soggy lump of paper in the ditch. I search the undercarriage of the car with a flashlight. I cry. I yell. I threaten the cookie gods with the shake of my fist that if they don't return the order form, I'll never purchase another fundraiser ever again.

Accepting defeat, I post a message on Facebook to please email me the amount of cookies each person ordered. Trusting the numbers are accurate, I divvy up each person's preferences into individual bags after three days of receiving emails from all those whom I'd pedaled. Yes, you read that correctly. I pedaled. Not my cute Girl Scout, but I.

Oh, take off your judgy-pants. It's faster and more efficient to set the order form out on the table at work and send out a blanket, "Hey, wanna buy some Girl Scout cookies?" and wait for the responses to pour in than it is to follow my kid around the neighborhood and wait for her to ring your doorbell and give her spiel. I'm defeating the purpose of her doing the selling. I know!

Coming home the next day, I open the door to discover my lard-butt Basset Hound has escaped her confined section of the house and has devoured several boxes of my nemesis: Peanut Butter Patties. She has consumed a whopping $44 worth of these treats and never puked once. Could have killed her myself if the chocolate consumption isn't going to do it.

What choice do I have but to truck back over to the facility to replace the ones eaten by the dang dog. Trying to outsmart the hungry hound, I store the replacement cookies in my trunk. All to be melted by the unusually hot March in Houston.

2. Truck back over to the facility to replace the goopy mess that used to be cookies. Ironically my irresponsible kid is the one who's supposed to be learning valuable life skills from this whole experience. The least I can do is make her bag up the orders we do have from the people who emailed us, although they clearly can't remember their exact order. Our numbers are all wrong! Some people receive more than they initially requested, while others get totally gypped and end up with not enough boxes.

3. Truck back over to the facility to replace the boxes inadvertently given to those who can't remember their original order and received someone else's orders instead. On day eight of this adventure, I now have to hide the cookies from the Basset, the sun, and my kids who keep opening boxes to nibble on. At four bucks a box, this is getting expensive! I have a new hiding spot where neither animals, nor heat, nor grubby little fingers can pillage the loot: the back of the closet.

Ready to deliver my last four orders—oops, did I say my last orders? I mean my daughter's orders, right? Whatever. I sneak around the obstacle course I created to hide the goods and catapult myself over the folding chairs to capture the last of the orders stowed in the back of the coat closet. Lugging the cardboard boxes filled to the brim with new cookies, I feel tiny pin pricks on my hands and arms. I climb through coats that have dislodged from their hangers, an old printer, and a plethora of scrapbook materials I've never had time to open. Making it to the doorway of the closet, my arms are stinging more and more. The light reveals hundreds, thousands of ants up my arms and swarming inside and outside of … Every.Freaking.Box.Of.Ruined.Girl.Scout.Cookies.

That's it. The ants are the last straw. The camel's back is broken. I fling box after box across the room, screaming with rage. Ants are flying. Cookies and patience are crumbling.

Tom's eyes stare in horror and he warns, "Kids, go upstairs before you get hurt. NOW!"

Thundering thuds pound up the staircase and little eyes poke through the blinds as they witness their mother open the front door screaming with rage, "I HATE GIRL SCOUT COOKIES! I HATE GIRL SCOUT COOKIES!" I shout and shout till the shout in me is gone.

I think it is pretty clear to my neighbors and those within hearing distance of the Teachers' Lounge that this little Girl Scout has quit.

Lesson Learned: The Girl Scout troop only receives 60-whopping-cents for every $4 box they sell. Next year, I will whip out my checkbook and just write a check for $50 to the leader and refuse to sell the actual cookies. My sanity and reputation with my neighbors are more important than a Thin Mint. Yep. That's my plan, and I'm sticking to it!

Hotter Than a Hooker at Church

Our church has a fall festival every year for the neighborhood. Everyone comes in costume, we have booths for the kids with a sinful amount of candy, bounce houses, and train rides. It's one of my favorite events we do each year toward community outreach.

Planning my costume is fun. I love Halloween and dressing up as something I'll never be in real life like a woodland fairy or a poufy pink princess. This year, I want something a little spunkier. Something with great make-up and maybe even a wig that will disguise my red locks. Not wanting to spend much money, I rifle through my closet and discover a red Japanese kimono my mother-in-law had bought me several years ago in hopes of my husband thinking it would be sexy in the bedroom.

Public Service Announcement: a mother-in-law should never purchase lingerie for her daughter-in-law to turn-on her son. Ever. And unless my husband is really into kinky Anime, which he isn't, a kimono won't ignite anything in the bedroom but some giggles.

Blowing the dust off the silk, I research hairstyles and make-up of Geishas and purchase a fabulous wig. Tom never asks what my costume will be, so I never mention it and just think a surprise will be more fun anyway. I stow away in the church restroom and begin my transformation into a Japanese goddess.

My face is caked with white foundation, my eyes are adorned with heavy black liquid eyeliner, and my lips are perfectly ruby-red. I can so rock being an Asian chick! I waddle my way out to our booth as if my feet are bound and pose next to my husband. He does a double take. A triple take.

"What in the world?"

I twirl to give the full effect. "A Geisha. I've always thought they're cool."

Shaking his head, "What part of being a Japanese hooker do you feel is appropriate at a family church event?"

A hooker? What? I recall Geishas were highly trained dancers, entertainers, calligraphers, artists, hostesses to elite society and to emperors, but hookers? Oh, wait. I do remember seeing the movie *Memoirs of a Geisha* and ... oh, crap! They did specialize in erotic sex.

Lovely.

All around me are my pint-size Sunday School students dressed as a T-Rex, Cinderella, and Batman, while I'm dressed as a prostitute. Paranoia is setting in as I imagine their parents gazing at me wondering if I am an appropriate person to teach their children about Jesus.

This carnival being an outreach to the community and those seeking a church home, we are thrilled when guests attend. But dang the luck, a group of visiting Japanese people are standing against a tree near my booth staring at me. Being gawked at is quite uncomfortable for me, especially as my husband gets the giggles. I give him a glare, and he says, "This is your fault, you know. They're staring because they don't know whether to take offense that you're dressed as an Asian or because you're dressed as a prostitute. Either way, it's not good."

Lesson Learned: In retrospect, I can't think of a better place for a hooker to be on a Sunday than at church seeking forgiveness. Prostitutes need God, too.

The Metaphorical "Kid"

It's difficult managing four dogs and two children at the veterinary clinic. So, I prefer taking two dogs for their appointment, run home, exchange them for the other two dogs, and drive back to the vet, sans kids. It's time consuming, but worth not having a headache later.

However, Tom has to coach a basketball game at school, so I have no choice—we are all headed to the appointment together. One big, happy family.

With a dog leash in each of my hands and a canine companion assigned to each kid to handle, we arrive like a three-ring circus. The vet walks into the examining room, and I explain, "So sorry I have to bring the whole crew at once. My husband has to work, so my little helpers are in tow."

Taylor's dog "Johnny Cash," named after his musical obsession, is the first to be examined. As the vet checks his ears, she replies, "No problem. I love having little helpers in here. Taylor, what does your dad do for a job?"

With a very serious face, Taylor answers, "He's a goat hunter." My eyes pop up to Dr. Baird. She sweetly smiles and corrects, "Oh. Do you mean he hunts deer?" Shaking his head back and forth, he replies, "No. He hunts goats in the mountains."

I retort, "Taylor, that isn't even close to being true! We live hours and hours away from any sort of mountain. Your dad is a P.E. teacher and a coach at the junior high. Tell Dr. Baird the truth."

Sticking to it, Taylor looks right in the doctor's eyes, "Yep. He's a goat hunter."

Lesson Learned: There are endless similarities between goats and junior high kids, such as the smell, the destructive messiness, and the difficulty in herding them. The metaphor is quite literary, actually. Taylor may have a future as an English professor at Purdue. Just go with it.

I'm Proud of My Fourth Grade Prostitute

My fourth-grade daughter is studying heroes of Texas history. Texans take extreme pride in our antiquity. Pride may be a mild word. We may actually utilize brainwashing techniques to secure the allegiance of young children to our Lone Star State.

Katy is assigned a research project in which she dresses up in costume to resemble her assigned historical figure and orally presents her report to both the class and the parents. Of all the luck, her assigned character is Emily West Morgan.

For those who aren't familiar with this character, Ms. Morgan was an indentured servant known for her beauty. During the Battle of San Jacinto in 1836, she was hired to go into the camp of Santa Anna, the enemy, and work her way into his private tent where she had sex with him while the Texas troops, led by General Sam Houston, ambushed and defeated the Mexican soldiers. Emily is hailed as the one responsible for securing our independence from Mexico by using her seductive charm. She is known as "The Yellow Rose of Texas" because her bi-racial heritage gave her skin a golden yellow tone. There have been several songs written and recorded about this twenty-year-old heroine. One version sung by Johnny Lee and Jane Brody became the title song to a TV show and ranked the number one country song in 1984. A random piece of trivia you'll never need to know.

During the research portion of the project, Katy becomes engrossed in websites about Emily West Morgan. However, her discoveries on the internet also raise A LOT of questions. Questions I'm not quite ready to tackle.

Being a teacher, I don't want to be one of those annoying moms who overreacts and shields her children into a life of naiveté, so I answer Katy's questions with honesty, but decide to email her teacher to see exactly how she wants us to approach the notion of using sex as a weapon. The teacher responds that she knows Katy is mature and responsible enough to handle the topic. She explains she has printed a bunch of information that Katy and I can edit at home to scrap any "inappropriate" information. Duh! Don't you think Katy is enthralled with the "inappropriate" information?! Those are the facts she wants to keep, not toss in the trash!

I reply to the email, asking for a new topic. She explains the other topics are all taken and there really aren't other female historical roles available, so my daughter will just have to do the best she can.

Okay. We'll deal with the research and focus on Emily obtaining her paperwork to be an indentured servant and how she travels with important military personnel during a difficult time in Texas history.

Now, onto the next problem: how in the world am I going to dress Katy up as a hired prostitute? I'm picturing her costume now and it isn't "appropriate". And if I skip over the hooker role, how will I dress her as an indentured slave while trying to remain politically correct? Nothing about this is "appropriate." I may just stick a yellow rose between her teeth and have her twirl a baton to the song "Yellow Rose of Texas" and just call it a day.

We decide to keep reading about Ms. Morgan to see if there are other aspects of her life we can steer the report toward. Research says that after sleeping with Santa Anna, she continued to sleep her way through prominent government officials and even ended up as the wife of the vice-president of the Republic of Texas.

Great. This bit of legend complicates the costume even more. Now, do I incorporate lots of flashy bling in the attire to represent her gold-digging tendencies toward escalating her wealth and status by means of her vagina? Is this the lesson Katy will learn? Sleep with the right men, honey, and you'll become the vice-president's wife?

Luckily, my Aunt Pam comes through with an authentic red and yellow prairie dress, circa mid-1800s. Bingo! For an English teacher, the colors couldn't have been more symbolic: yellow for the nickname of the heroine and red for the lust she instilled and the blood shed at the battle.

In regard to how her heroine earned her fame, Katy remembers learning how to play a specific domino game the previous summer with her cousins, so she decides to say in her oral report, "Emily West Morgan enjoyed having fun and playing games. So, she went into Santa Anna's tent and played a mean game of Mexican Train with him while our boys defeated the enemy." She couldn't have been more accurate! Ha!

I receive a lot of raised eyebrows from parents sitting in the room regarding "Mexican Train," but the kids appear clueless and applaud with glee at the conclusion of the report. Katy earns her "A" on the report, learns some history, and gets to wear a cool dress. Sounds like a good day to me!

Lesson Learned: Usually, I learn from these strange experiences. However, I think this particular lesson learned should be dedicated to the teacher who assigned this topic to a ten-year-old who discovered that sex can have financial rewards and can lead to becoming famous. Not much has changed in modern time. Texas Curse: may this teacher get that 1984 twangy song stuck in her head that will play on a continuous loop for the rest of her life!

This Requires How Much Butter?

Our family loves to celebrate holidays and special occasions for all 30 of our family members. Even at the age of 85, my grandmother can still host a fabulous Christmas dinner. With the help of her yellow legal pad and a pencil, she divvies out the food assignments without first consulting any of us about our preference or specialty, but once the dish is written on the pad, it stays.

Much to my dismay, I'm assigned mashed potatoes. This gets tricky for someone who does not make homemade mashed potatoes, but certainly enjoys critiquing other's attempts at this starchy indulgence. For our family's palate, if the mashed potatoes are bland, the whole meal is therefore just average, even if the rest of the food rocks. However, if the taters are scrumptious, then it adds bonus points to the meal, even if the rest of the food is just so-so. The pressure is on!

Not wanting to disappoint four generations of family members, I spend time researching recipes. After reading many reviews, I settle on Paula Dean's garlic mashed potatoes. Now being born and raised in Texas, I love southern cooking, but holy calories!

Running behind schedule as usual, my sweet husband and kids come in to offer me help when they see me crying from squirting freshly pressed garlic directly in my eye (ouch!). Panic ensues while under the pressure of the clock while temporarily blinded. Tom peels potatoes, Katy slices them into chunks, and Taylor plops them into the boiling water. We have quite an assembly line going on.

Making conversation, Tom asks, "Where did you get this recipe?"

With mascara streaming down my garlic-infused eye, "Paula Dean."

As Tom blends the potatoes into perfection, he inquires, "Now, who is Paula Dean? Does she sit near us at church?"

Both kids and I stare at him in silence. There are no words.

What a blasphemous thing to ask while standing in a kitchen in the South! Now, pass the butter, y'all!

Lesson Learned: Strangely, regular church goers seem to claim their pew. Without fail, they can be found in the same spot every Sunday. Although we've sat in the same spot for over a decade, I still can't depend on Tom to remember the names of those around us. Even if we've shared a meal with them that includes mashed potatoes. Clueless.

Sweating in Hell but Hoping for Heaven

While picking at his dinner plate in disgust, Taylor says, "Mom, I hope in Heaven, asparagus doesn't taste like poop, like it does here on Earth."

Yes, Taylor, I hope a lot of things in Heaven are different than they are here on this planet.

I hope in Heaven my butt-cheeks don't look like the surface of the moon.

I hope in Heaven Nutella is calorie-free. Nutella. The sole reason my tush has craters and caverns enough to make Neil Armstrong long for another trip to the moon.

I hope in Heaven that thigh-friction doesn't exist when I walk.

I hope in Heaven to never discover another grey pubic hair.

I hope in Heaven the toothpaste doesn't fall off the toothbrush and plop in the sink when I get it wet under the stream of water.

I hope in Heaven I won't sneeze when I apply mascara. (Angels wear make-up, right?)

And I hope in Heaven crotch-sweat is non-existent.

You know what I'm talking about. The kind of moisture you can feel bead up at the lower-back and trickle down the back of your thigh. The kind of sweat where I pick the cotton-blend dress in the perfect shade of blue to wear with kick-ass heels for a job interview with a team of administrators during the month of Hades ... I mean, during the month of July. July in Houston is what is described in the last book of the Bible, Revelation: an unquenchable, forever-burning pit of fire.

Sweat. July. The heels. The dress.

The kind of fashion ensemble that when I put it on says to the world, "I own you. Bow to the legs." The kind of dress that can rock a board room. And the kind of dress that when I stand up to shake hands after an hour-long, nerve-racking interview humiliatingly displays sweat in the outline of my panties and the outline of my double-D bra.

In Heaven, I hope there is no crotch or boob sweat.

Lesson Learned: Always wear black to an interview and slather antiperspirant in alllll the hidden spots. And pray I make it to Heaven.

Oh, Goodness Snakes Alive!

The love of Taylor's life is what makes most moms scream with horror and stand on a chair for safety—rats. Not cute little mice. Not a fluffy hamster. But the beady-eyed, long hairless tailed kind of rat. Three of them: Luke, Max, and Sparkles.

After Taylor repeatedly places one of these rodents on my shoulder for safe keeping as he runs to the restroom or plops it on my lap while he ties his shoe, I've grown quite fond of the little creepers. I will even give the rats credit for helping Taylor become a better reader. Max, in particular, sweetly sits on top of his head while Taylor does his reading homework. Patiently and without criticism, Max perches and listens attentively, which is more than I can claim for myself.

Taylor also loves snakes. I can handle the rat, but the idea of snake makes me yearn for a new reptile-skin purse, belt, or boots—not a pet. So for his eighth birthday party, Taylor asks for a snake party. Thirty snakes in my living room to be exact. I spend days researching cool-looking cakes to shape like a snake. Hoping for chocolate, Taylor denies me and wants red velvet so when we hack into it, the inside of the cake-snake looks bloody. I can guarantee I will not be munching on any such confection. Gross.

My checklist is almost complete: Taylor has a cobra t-shirt to wear, my heel-tips of my snake-skin boots are repaired so I fit in with the theme, the gummy snakes and stuffed animal snakes are purchased for party favors, and I call to verify the snake-party-dude is still planning on showing up.

"Snakes by Jake, how may I help you?"

"Hi. This is Kasey Brooks. Y'all are booked for my son's party this Saturday. He is sooo excited! He even told me about a dream he had last night about his party. He dreamed a snake got loose, slithered its way to his bedroom and ate his pet rats."

"WHAT? He has pet rats?"

"I know, I know. They're disturbing to look at, but they really are quite sweet."

"I don't doubt that, but I'm concerned. Several of our snakes swallow rats whole. If the ten-foot pythons smell even a small trace of a rat on your son or any of his guests, they'll take his hand completely off."

"Are you SERIOUS?"

"I would never joke about this. This could be a disaster of a celebration if your son is maimed during his party."

(Stunned silence at picturing this scenario and visualizing twenty boys witnessing this event and screaming in mass chaos.)

The lady continues, "Well, the good news is that the party is still 36 hours away. Pick out his clothing right now, wash it in the hottest water you can find, and do not allow him to enter his bedroom for 24 hours prior to the party. Make him shower and scrub his arms and hands really well before the party starts."

(More stunned silence)

"Ma'am, are you still there?"

"Umm. I'm here. Just busy picking my jaw up from the floor. I am so glad I called to confirm. That could have been a rat-tastrophe!"

Lesson Learned: As much as I loathe Chuck E. Cheese, the mascot is a large rodent. Next year, forget any party with live animals. We're headed to eat pizza with a pimply-faced teenager with bad body odor in a mascot costume instead.

May I Just Lick You So It'll Rub Off On Me?

With the mortgage loan rates being so low, we have chosen to refinance our house. After we collect the necessary documentation, the doorbell rings, and we open the door to a dead-ringer for Morgan Freeman. When he walks in our home, we are stunned at the uncanny resemblance. There is something about this actor ... and the mortgage dude ... that strikes awe.

We close the door behind him, and in a half-whisper/half-sign-language communication, we ponder the chance this might really be the real Mr. Freeman. Deciding he's much too young and probably only 50 years old at best, we invite him to sit at the kitchen table, pour him some tea, and begin crunching numbers. Katy begins circling the man like a shark stalking a gushing wound. She sneaks from corner to corner of the house leering in his direction, pointing behind him and whispering, "Mom! That's the guy who plays God in the movie *Bruce Almighty* ... He's. In. Our. House!"

Throughout the two-hour process, Katy requests his autograph, tries to nonchalantly touch his arm, and offers him innumerable juice boxes, which he politely declines. In between our signatures on papers that we'll never fully read or understand, Mock-Morgan tells us he has just turned eighty years old. WHAT?

Seeing our shock and desire to know the location of the fountain of youth or the plastic surgeon he uses, he must have read our minds. He says he attributes his youthful energy to marrying a woman half a century younger and having a child recently with her. Okay, now I also need the doctor's phone number who must prescribe a bulk amount of the little blue pill to him. Wowzers. Fake-Freeman then comments his toddler-aged daughter loves playing with his great-grandkids while he is at Zumba class.

I didn't know whether to high-five him, give him a condom, or sign up for Zumba.

Lesson Learned: Stalk the dude. Become his muse. Find his secrets to youth, vitality, and moisturizer cream.

Woman of the Evening

I'm not a fan of surprises. I get a thrill out of making a very specific wish list for special occasions. I'm even guilty of buying my own gifts, wrapping them in beautiful paper and bows, writing "To Kasey" on the tags, and placing them secretly under the Christmas tree.

However, Tom loves to shop for me. Sometimes this is successful. Other times, not so much. Offering to grocery shop relieves my stress, but his choice of tampons causes me to waddle like a penguin.

His knack at buying bananas is baffling. Why is it men must choose the longest bananas in the bunch? Do they think it's some sort of psychological foreplay? A Freudian nine-inch phallic fruit is superfluous. I'm quite comfortable with six inches, thank you very much.

Quite often, Tom has great taste. He can pick out a fabulous handbag and elegant earrings, but when it comes to purchasing clothes, we clearly have differing tastes. I prefer to cover the lumps, bumps, and humps. He enjoys dressing me like a twenty-two-year-old, high-dollar hooker.

The ill-fitting, generic brand of a tampon, I can grin and bear. The completely backless dress that may or may not double as a long blouse is not appropriate for a forty-year-old with a few straggly gray eyebrow hairs and breasts that demand to be imprisoned in a wired contraption.

Although his sentiment is heartfelt (and hormonally-charged), I decide to exchange the dress for something more suited to my years and wisdom. At the store, I gather other options and head to the fitting room. A knock lightly raps at the door, so I answer, "Yes?"

On the other side, the saleswoman's voice says, "Hi. I remember your husband coming in to purchase the dress you are returning. I've been married thirty-six years, so I feel the need to share some advice with you in regard to husbands."

I peek my head out and keep my naked-self concealed behind the door. "Umm … okay."

"When he picked out the dress last week, he told me how beautiful you'd look in it."

"No offense to your merchandise, but when I'm wearing it, I look like I'm trying to sell my goodies. I can't wear this in public. If I need a bikini wax to wear what masquerades itself as a dress, then it's too dang short."

"You need to trust me on this. He bought this especially for you. He thinks you are gorgeous, so swallow your pride and wear it for him."

Feeling guilty, I put my own clothes back on, agree to keep the dress, and head back home to hang it in my closet. The next night, we arrange for a babysitter and discuss a restaurant suitable to celebrate our anniversary. Knowing I don't want any of my high school students to see me wearing this contraption made of intertwining red dental floss disguised as a dress, I suggest we eat somewhere different than our usual haunts … somewhere far, far away … free from any eyes that might recognize me … and the tramp-stamp peeking around the material I can't even wear normal panties with.

Thirty miles away amongst the skyscrapers of downtown Houston, we finish a very romantic dinner at a French restaurant. We meander outside where Tom scoops me up to where my tip-toes barely touch the ground and kisses me with gusto. In mid slurp, I hear, "Mrs. Brooks, is that you??"

Horrified, I turn to see two of the boys in my fifth period American Literature class snapping a picture with their cell phones, originally thinking they are capturing a photo of a hooker on the corner. We make eye contact. Their mouths fall open as they realize it's their nipply-no-bra-wearing, tattoo-sporting, prostitute-garbed teacher making out with a man on the corner of Main Street.

Lesson Learned: To the saleswoman: you're wrong, lady. Bras, normal underwear, and something that zips all the way to the nape of the neck are totally okay! If you want to wear the hoochy apparel, more power to ya, but this chick is covering up her chicklets.

He Ain't ~~Heavy~~ Gummy, He's My Brother

Taylor comes home from school, slings his thirty-thousand-pound backpack on the sofa, and heads to the fridge to grab a snack. I ask, "How was school?"

I receive the usual shrug. "Fine."

Annoyed by this generic answer, I persist, "Anything good or bad happen?"

"Nope. Just a usual day." As he turns to sprawl across the oversized-chair, I see a chunk of his hair is missing. A broad bald-patch proves that something interesting must have happened in his day because I didn't send him to school in the same condition. He touches it, then shrugs like it's no big deal.

My verbose Katy pipes up, "On the bus this morning, a kid threw gum and it landed in Taylor's hair. I tried to pull it out, which was gross. It got all smashed up in his hair, so I told him we'd have to cut it out."

At this point, I'm giving her the look.

She continues, "So, I ask my friend Sage if she has any scissors in her backpack, which she didn't. I remembered the bus driver used scissors one time when cutting out a new nametag for a student, so I ran down the aisle to ask to borrow them."

I inquire, "The bus was at a complete stop before you got up to go ask him, right?"

"No. We were still moving to the next pick-up area."

"I hope you got in trouble for running while the bus was in motion."

"Nope. I never get in trouble for it."

"So this happens often?"

(Shoulder shrug) "I guess. So, anyway, I got the scissors from the bus driver and ran back to Taylor."

"You ran with scissors while the bus was moving?"

"Uh, huh. But when I ran with them, I pointed them downward like you taught me. A few times, like when the bus would make a turn, I'd tumble on top of another kid, but no one got hurt."

My eyes bulge, and I gasp as I picture my child blinding another kid with a sharp pointy object.

"When I get back to Taylor, I try to cut just a small piece where the gum got smushed. But we hit a bump when I was trying to snip which is why I accidentally cut a much larger chunk than I meant to."

"I see that. In Native American terms, it looks like you scalped my papoose."

"No blood, no foul," she chirps (she also receives The Look a second time). "Then, I ran the scissors back up to the bus driver and used my manners when I said 'Thanks!' and ran back to sit down."

"So, you ran on a moving bus ... with scissors ... four times? And your bus driver never stopped you?"

Katy corrects me, "Two with scissors and two without. Nah ... We're cool like that."

Lesson Learned: Maybe ignorance is bliss. When my kid comes home and shrugs in apathy as I ask about his day, it's okay to stay in the dark so I don't add more gray hair to my own scalp.

What's Your Emergency?

I've noticed lately that women have one rectangular breast, which is usually the left one, and one regularly shaped breast, usually on the right side, ranging from round to oblong. I'm fascinated by this. Clearly, the rectangular boob is created not from a genetic disorder but rather from a cell phone. Honestly, when a preschool-aged child can learn shapes from boobs instead of *Sesame Street*, it's time for an intervention for women to refrain from using their bras as phone cradles.

I guess I'm somewhat obsessed with bodily shapes. My boobs are just fine, but my butt suffers from the ancestral disease called "Noassatall." To create a vision of a fuller bum, instead of carrying my phone in my bra like many women I see, I carry it in my back pocket. It's a balancing act: a phone on one side and my metal credit card/driver's license carrier on the other. Equal size, equal shape, with my shirt hanging an inch below the top part of the rectangle to mask odd outlines.

Needing to run a quick errand, I slide my supplies in my two back pockets and head to the jewelry counter at JC Penney's to get my watch fixed. My cell phone rings (as I kind of enjoy a titillating vibration). I answer. On the other end, I hear, "Ma'am? Are you safe?"

Confused, I reply, "Umm, yeah."

The mysterious, but very serious voice, asks, "Are you in a safe location?" Racking my brain trying to figure out who the heck this person is, respond, "Well, I'm getting my watch battery replaced at a department store, so I think I'm pretty safe. Who is this?"

The all business-no-bull voice barks, "This is the Harris County Police Dept. You called 911. Are you in danger?"

Stunned silence. The only audible sound is my heartbeat racing a mile a minute. Oh, crap! I've heard they fine you money for mistakes like this. I respond back to the androgynous voice, "Umm...I must have butt-dialed 911. I'm so sorry. I have no idea how that happened."

How *does* that happen? How does one's booty dial the specific numbers 9-1-1 and then hit send? That's quite acrobatic if you think about it. Looks like I might take this little freaky side-show of mine with my square butt cheeks and audition for *America's Got Talent*.

Lesson Learned: Use a purse, not a pocket or bra. A good handbag is much more attractive than rectangular T&A. Plus, it'll keep you outta trouble with the law.

Work It, Girl (Scout)

My favorite event my daughter's Girl Scout troop participates in is the annual Father-Daughter dance. Picking out a pretty dancing dress that twirls when she spins and seeing my husband put the corsage on her wrist and escort her into the car just warms my heart. Every girl should be so blessed to have a dad who truly loves having fun with his daughter.

I did not have this experience as a kid. My mom was my Girl Scout leader for many years, and she rocked at it! However, my date was usually my uncle, surely coaxed into it by my mom so I could attend the dance. My dad was always M.I.A. that night either spending the evening with his mistress or sitting in cell block 87. For real. I don't think I'm emotionally scarred by it because I'm thankful my uncle took me, but seeing my husband participate in this event with my daughter makes it that much more special to me.

Now that I'm the mother and no longer the daughter/niece, I help by serving cookies and punch where I enjoy seeing fathers trying to get their swerve on and daughters skipping around without their shoes, getting the bottom of their pantyhose dirty. This makes me smile.

Usually, the typical party songs are played. It's hysterical to watch these 40-year-old men get excited and drag their daughters to the dance floor to show off their moves to songs like "YMCA," "The Chicken Song," and "Cupid Shuffle," and sweet to see them pick up their little girls in their arms to slow dance to songs like "I Hope You Dance." However, this year there is a different DJ who looks a bit shady with his slicked-back hair poking out from a fedora and armpit-hair peeking out of a stained tank top.

Sure enough, the men awkwardly dance with their tiny tulled-skirted partners to heart-warming family classics like "You Shook Me All Night Long," "Dirty Girl," and "Shake It for Me." As the little girls with ringlets wiggle their booties and shimmy their shoulders, the dads' faces change from a let's-dance-with-our-daughter-in-a-fun-silly-way to oh-lordy-I-can-only-picture-my-eighteenth-birthday-at-the-strip-club-when-Chastity-twirled-her-tassels-counterclockwise-to-the-beat. The last thing a dad wants to hear while spinning his little girl is a song that has the potential to give him wood while picturing a woman in clear stiletto heels and a bedazzled thong.

Without delay, the dance floor is a mass exodus of fathers dragging their gyrating princesses OFF the dance floor and over to the cookie table.

Here's a clue, Mr. DJ: If a song you want to play has ever been introduced by a sleazy man in the microphone booth with, "Gentlemen, Bambi will be performing on stage 2," then maybe you shouldn't play it at a Girl Scout event. The girls don't earn patches on their sash for pole dancing, dude.

Lesson Learned: Do a better job of interviewing the DJ next time. If his resume includes establishments called Treasures or Baby-Ohh's, then he might not be the best choice for a Father-Daughter dance. And men, stop wearing fedoras. Gross.

Welcome to the Neighborhood!

Finally, it's late November, which means it is now permissible to jog outside without having a heat stroke. Living in Houston, it is a rare evening when I can crank up my 80s rock on my iPod and head outside to exercise around our new neighborhood.

I usually look around to make sure the coast is clear before I break out into my Phoebe from the TV show *Friends* method of running with my arms flailing, legs running like an injured gazelle. Running like this with wild abandonment makes me actually enjoy exercise (is that an oxymoron?). In this quiet neighborhood, I feel immense satisfaction at working out without the stares from judging eyes like in a gym.

On this particular night, my "me time" doesn't go as expected as I take off through the neighborhood, meandering through the streets, and creating a mental map of how each street is connected to the next street before I become completely lost. As I round the corner to Rolling Lakes Drive and notice no one is standing outside of their house to witness me, I go full-force-Phoebe, knowing that it will make me laugh on the inside to experience such crazy flailing of my limbs. I've heard laughing burns a ton of calories, so a good guffaw while running is sure to make my jiggly parts shrink faster. I highly recommend it.

Six houses down, as I pass the garage, a lady peeks at me with a confused expression while watching my display. I'm afraid she thinks I've escaped from the residential home for mentally deranged that is just two miles from our house. A slight wave, a shrug of the shoulders, and I zoom past, not worrying too much about what she really thinks.

On the route back to my house, my exertion has gotten my insides functioning a tad too well, and I realize I'll have to do something extremely unladylike any second. Looking to the right, the coast is clear. Looking to the left, no one is in hearing distance, so while jamming to the song "Hey, Mickey" by Toni Basil, I allow a gust of wind at hurricane strength to escape from my clenched gluteal muscles. Yep, I pull that off quite nicely, until …

You see, every male and a heck-of-a-lot of females in our part of Texas own a truck. Not just any pick-up variety, but a jacked-up truck with an extended cab and tires big enough to support King Kong.

Looping my way off the sidewalk to oonch past the truck bed after my loud expulsion, I hear laughter. As I pass, I see six men who are our new neighbors sitting on lawn chairs on the other side of the truck who had definitely heard the various octaves of my toooot. I give a little half-smile, a quick wave, and run faster than I ever have to escape the high-fives and head nods of utter respect for my loud flatulence.

Welcome to the neighborhood. Nice to meet you. Yep, I live three doors down.

Lesson Learned: If I can impress a group of redneck men drinking beer in their driveway, then dang girl, I may need to alter my diet a bit.

Don't Make Me Hurt You

We live in a world of acronyms: ADHD (Attention Deficit/Hyperactivity Disorder), IRS (Internal Revenue Service), DUI (Driving Under the Influence), etc. I could go on forever.

We also live in a world of internet shopping. Amazon.com has saved what little sanity I have left. With a couple of clicks from my mouse, I can have my entire Christmas list for fifteen people bought and delivered without having to battle the Houston traffic or the pajama-pant-wearing crowd at Wal-Mart.

We are used to our mail-dude leaving our packages on our front doorstep, nestled between the bricks and our bushes so they're hidden from thieving eyes on the street. So when the doorbell rings, this is unusual. Hollering from the kitchen for Katy to answer the door while I'm trying to stop the overflowing boiling water, she runs to answer it.

I hear her muffled words and then she bellows for me loudly enough for the neighbors to hear, "Mom, CPS is at the door and wants to talk to you." My heart sinks. Why on earth would Child Protective Services be at my door? Was I reported for the meltdown I'd had in the front yard when I stepped on the Christmas lights and shattered the bulbs? Was I reported when I sent my kids to school in t-shirts and basketball shorts in thirty degree weather without a coat? Did the neighbors report us for my kids having bruises up and down their legs from kicking the crap out of each other? Did they witness my meltdown on the patio regarding Girl Scout cookies? Great.

With my heart in my throat and my driver's license in my hand for identification purposes, I amble to the door, afraid for my future. When I step onto the porch, the man in uniform is not from CPS but from UPS (United Postal Service)!

After signing for my package, I shut the door and say, "Katy! You scared me to death! That was UPS, not CPS!"

"Same thing," she replies and skips back upstairs without a care in the world.

If I hadn't already had visions of CPS taking away my kids and placing them in foster care, I would have killed my kid for this scare!

Lesson Learned: Katy's weekend homework is to thoroughly research the difference between these two acronyms and write about it in a well-developed five-paragraph essay. She'll be learning the lesson this time.

Don't Hassle the Hound

I've heard owners and their dogs share a physical resemblance. If this is true, why do people intentionally choose ugly dogs? Bulgy eyes. Smashed up noses. Tails that don't discreetly cover the booty-hole. Gross. Since every bit of rumor, legend, and theory has a little bit of truth imbedded in it somewhere, I don't want to risk looking like a Bulldog—droopy, wrinkly, and just as wide as I am tall. No, thanks.

If my dog and I are bound to morph into one another's corporeal essence, I have a method for choosing my pet. I want a dog with a big chest, tiny waist, and legs as long as a mile. Sounds like a Greyhound to me!

When I arrive at the Greyhound adoption shelter, I always have in mind a beautiful, blond, long-n-lean, lovely female with good manners and a sassy strut. However, what I choose and what chooses me are totally different. Instead, I leave the facility with a black male with scars covering his fat body. Yes, ordinarily, the words fat and Greyhound are oxymorons.

"Bullet" was used as target practice by hunters who trespassed on the training farm where these dogs learn to race. These men thought they'd get in a few practice shots on moving targets before setting out to find deer. There is a special place in Hell for people like this. Once named for his speed, Bullet is now branded with the name that gives evidence to the twenty-three exit wounds that miraculously escaped his vital organs. My new dog may be filled with buckshot, but he has a spirit of a champ.

With all my might, I hoist his body into my car. He'd discovered a love for food while recovering at an animal hospital. No longer running off the calories, he developed a bit of a tummy, which is quite an anomaly to see on this breed. He also has a thyroid condition, which doesn't help his tubby-self. At 126-whopping-pounds, Bullet is given a fresh start at life—on my couch.

Bullet's sweet nature has inspired me to volunteer with Greyhound Pets of America once a month, which is rewarding. I love helping these dogs, and to be honest, if the adage is true about owners resembling their dogs, I feel like the more time I spend with this breed, the more my body might resemble their sleek form.

It worked. I now have a gut to match Bullet's. This isn't how the metamorphosis is supposed to happen!

The first Saturday of the month offers a cool opportunity for Bullet and me. We are asked to participate with twenty other Greyhounds at a training session where veterinarians from around the country travel to Houston to learn pet-acupuncture. Although our own dogs are never pricked like a hairy pin cushion, their lean physique and exquisite musculature help the doctors visually see the exact spot to place the medicated barbs.

Bullet and I waddle in together, share a complimentary croissant with honey butter (don't judge) and park our big butts on the carpet outside the examination room where the vets take their final licensing exam. I feel the stare of an underweight-by-choice female doctor, one who clearly embodies beauty and brains. Not only am I being judged for each bite of carbs I devour, but my dog is receiving the stink-eye from her, too.

Before it is our turn, my three cups of morning coffee are yelling at me to release them from my bladder. In the stall, I overhear a conversation between two female examinees:

"Did you see the size of that fat-ass Greyhound? What idiot allows her dog to get that rotund? With my luck, that's the dog that'll be assigned to me for my testing. Gross. I can't see a single muscle on that thing!"

Yes. I hate her at this moment. She looks like the blond personified Greyhound I've always wanted to embody. A fat gram has clearly never stuck to her skinny butt.

The second vet continues Carmex-ing her lips, adjusts her cargo pants, and shrugs in agreement.

Annoyed ... okay, not just annoyed. My ~~feathers~~ cellulite is ruffled. This vet doesn't know what all my sweet boy has been through. His thyroid pill covered in an extra dollop of peanut butter surely isn't a crime. Has she never heard it is not right to judge a book by its cover? This Miss America-throw-back is begging for a lesson on why it's wrong to ridicule based on outward beauty alone. Okay, I admit it. Maybe I'm flashing back to the locker room in 7th grade. Brutal on a chubby girl.

Making my way back to the dog area, I see Little Ms. Bubble-Belly-Bigot sashay her way to the testing table. A balding vet who looks way too much like Inspector Clouseau randomly calls Bullet's assigned number. Together we heave ourselves up, hold back our proud shoulders, and flounce right up to the table. I cock my head and give a snarky smirk, "Luck's not on your side. In Bullet's defense, he has a thyroid issue. I hope you're nicer to your clients than you were in the restroom about my sweet dog who is volunteering his time to help *you* pass your test. You'll have to know the information based on knowledge—not on how well you can visibly see the muscles and tendons of a thin Greyhound. May the force be with you on your exam."

I hand her the leash, watch her struggle to lift my pudgy-pooch onto the table, and begin to sweat droplets of defeat.

Lesson Learned: Always watch what you say in the restroom in front of strangers. It may come back to bite you in the butt. If we resemble our dogs, embody one with a good heart ... not an over-groomed "bitch." Pick your breed and your judgments wisely.

If You Can't Fix Crazy, You Can at Least Clean It First

I hear laughter coming from the doorway into the garage where I'm being watched. Not just watched, but mocked. I turn around to see my husband shaking his head in disbelief through chuckles for what he is witnessing. "What are you doing?" he asks.

With rag in hand in 102 degree heat, I fire back, "I'm polishing some old, broken furniture before it goes to the curb because I don't want the trash men to think we are a dirty family."

This is no different than me trimming the dog's fur before I take her to the groomer so she doesn't think I'm a bad pet owner. Or scrubbing the sticky fingerprints off the windows of the backseat before I take my car to be detailed. Or washing my hair before I go to the salon so they think I always have a clean scalp. Or filing and painting my nails before I go to the manicurist. Or taking a water pill before stepping on the scale at my Weight Watchers meeting. Or scrubbing the toilet before the maid arrives.

Lesson Learned: I need therapy. But then I'd have to fix my mental stability before sitting on the shrink's couch.

Mistaken for a Pawn Star

On my bucket list is a trip to New England during autumn. Seeing paintings and photographs of the colorful fall leaves is beautiful, but seeing them in person would be so much better. In Texas, we only have two seasons: summer and almost-summer. Neither of these two seasons includes beautiful leaves.

My wish comes true when my cousin proposes to sweet Melissa who is from Connecticut.

October rolls around, a season of great boots, clothing that compliments my red hair and pale skin, and a wedding for our family! My grandmother, mom, and I catch a flight to a place whose landscape captivates me by its natural beauty. I just imagine God hand-painting each and every leaf for our enjoyment.

Needing to grab some dinner but too exhausted for a sit-down meal, the three of us decide to swing by Boston Market near our hotel for some take-out. With my Grandmother needing a walker and my Mom just having had knee-replacement surgery, it is easier for me to hop out of the backseat and run inside to order for us.

After finishing our food requests and paying for it, I step over to the fountain drink dispensers to fill our cups. An older couple enters the establishment and witnesses me struggling with three bags of food, my fabulous new fall-colored boots, and three large drinks. I am impressed to see that manners and chivalry are not only a part of the south as they approach me with a smile and offer to help me to the car since I'm juggling too much.

The only sentence that escapes my mouth is, "No, thanks. I'm fine."

The seventy-something-year-old man shrieks, "You're from Texas!"

Turning back with surprise, I reply, "How on earth do you know that just from one statement?" I mean, it's not like I was hollering the words, "Yee-Haw!" or even, "Howdy, partners!" It was just a simple, "No, thanks. I'm fine." How Texan can that possibly be?

His wife nods in agreement, as he explains, "Because you sound *just like* the people on that reality TV show *Texas Pawn Stars.*"

I don't think is this necessarily a positive compliment. Yes, I'm very proud of my Lone Star State, but I'm not sure I want to be branded by a quick reply as I'm walking out of a fast food joint. And I definitely don't want to sound like anyone hanging out at a pawn store all day long. Yikes.

Lesson Learned: Begin looking for linguistic classes to flatten my southern drawl, y'all.

Mum's the Word

I feel God hand picks some of the students I meet. Having taught many levels of English, from Mensa geniuses to those who struggle academically, all the way from 7th to 12th grade, every now and then a kid will mosey in my classroom and I immediately know God collided our two lives together for a reason. Usually, compassion and patience seem to be the common denominator when I reflect upon these special students.

Mark has some issues. He is the smartest kid on the planet, but he struggles socially. I seem to have developed a reputation in the building for working well with kids who have this particular problem. I hate labeling a kid with a disorder because we all have a situation we struggle with that attaches a label to us in some fashion or another. So, I'll just simply label him as a great kid.

A day doesn't go by without reversing the role of me being the student and Mark being the teacher, schooling his classmates and me in specialized topics like frogs and coins. During our year together, I learn every minute fact about these topics, and someday, if I'm sitting on a cruise ship playing a trivia game, I hope to get a question about frogs or coins because I'll rock the dock with my answers, thanks to Mark!

The high school where I teach has an obnoxious amount of team spirit with Homecoming being the most exciting event of the year. Mark is fully aware of this and enjoys participating, although I'm certain he's never had a date. Homecoming is a huge deal in Texas. In fact, we have relatives who live in Pennsylvania who came to visit during high school football season and one of the sightseeing activities they wanted to experience during their visit was to see the giant mums the girls wear to the homecoming football game. To give you a visual, the flower in the middle is a white mum about six inches in diameter. Sometimes there will be several mums attached together, depending on how much money is spent, which ranges from $90-$400. No, I'm not kidding. The planning of the mum is quite an undertaking and the struggle to pay for the mum is evident when a month before the game, high school boys can be seen going door-to-door asking neighbors if they can mow the lawn or pressure-wash the driveway for extra cash.

Connected to the mum are streams of ribbons about five feet long, often causing bloopers, bruises, and bumps on its tripping victim. Blinking lights, small stuffed animals, tiny bottles of bubbles, and an annoying collection of cow bells create quite a raucous environment while trying to teach *Julius Caesar*. It's fun to see and hear the mums for about an hour, but after my coffee-high wears off, the incessant ringing of bells is worse than Chinese water torture.

I wear my school spirit shirt to show support and enter my classroom to find Mark standing there with a huge mum with my name displayed in 2-inch glitter letters down one streamer and his name down the other. Truly touched by this sentiment, I pin it on. Securing it is a feat equivalent to climbing Mt. Everest by the time you pin twenty heavy-duty safety pins to your clothing, bra, and depending upon how heavy it is, tie it around the neck and shoulders for extra support, a good lathery sweat is worked up. I thank Mark and give him a side-hug. Side-hugs are something I've mastered because a full-frontal hug on a high school boy is beyond icky.

Four hours of school pass as I jingle my way through the lesson. After lunch, three girls sneak down to my classroom to inform me that it might be a good idea if I remove my mum because Mark thinks I am his date to the homecoming game and dance.

WHAT??

Just to clarify and keep my name out of the local newspaper, I call his mom. A mom whom I respect immensely and who sweetly sends me $5 Starbuck gift cards tucked inside heartfelt thank you cards to show her appreciation for being patient with her son. She explains the conversation a week ago when she took Mark to the florist to pay for my mum. Mark doesn't really think I am his date, but he is worried I'd be the only girl in the classroom who doesn't receive a big corsage. He doesn't want me to feel left out and sad.

Tears.

Again, Mark is morphing into the teacher-role, instructing me on compassion and consideration for others. After the day is over, I proudly display the mum on the wall by my desk for years afterward as a reminder to make others feel special and included just as Mark made me feel.

Lesson Learned: Some days I ponder, what if we had a world full of Marks? What a kind and compassionate world we'd have. No war. No hate. Just acceptance and kindness ... and lots of frog talk.

The Event in My Life That'll Earn Me a Shiny Crown in Heaven

Tom's 93-year-old grandmother, Helen, is a piece of work. She's been kicked out of seven nursing homes and all three of her children have tried to have her live with them, but they all boosted her crazy butt out the door too. Even in her younger years, she was impossible, nagging, harsh, and an all-around toot.

On Easter, a day symbolic of resurrection, Helen, has also been resurrected—right into our home. The Colorado social worker at the other end of the telephone explains that Helen has been evicted once again. Since none of her children will take her back and she's already spread her evil through the nursing homes in the area, the only option is to turn her over to the state.

I wouldn't turn my worst enemy over to a state nursing home. My mushy heart can't handle this. How wicked could this woman really be? I've heard stories from every member of my husband's extended family, but come on. How bad could it be? To answer this question, her name perfectly suits her, but it should be spelled: HELLen. This 93 year-old surely can't do much damage … nor live much longer.

Tom researches home renovation and builds walls to enclose a bedroom in our home. We ship her furniture and fly her down to live with us in Texas.

After watching her yell racial obscenities to the men who drove her furniture from Denver to Houston, I know we're in for a crazy adventure.

Helen is convinced our little black terrier is Satan whose mission is to possess her with evil spirits and suck her soul out of her body. If only we'd been that fortunate.

She whispers to the Schnauzer, whom she thinks is an angel in a fur suit, "Go find help! Satan is going to kill me!" and releases her to the neighborhood like she's Lassie seeking help for Timmy who'd fallen down the well. Thanks to her, we are frequent flyers at animal control, paying top dollar to spring our impounded dog out of jail for roaming the neighborhood. How many times can we explain to the officer that this Schnauzer is only trying to seek a neighbor to save Helen's soul from the demonic terrier?

Helen does have to tolerate my eight-year-old Katy, whom she nicknamed "Tramp," "Whore," and "Jezebel," and her myriad of giggling girlfriends, who enjoy playing tricks on the one whom they revengefully dubbed the "Wicked Witch of East-Texas."

The girls call her name in the lowest pitch they can make in their throat while strobing the lights, "Helllllen … Helllllen … " trying to resemble the voice of God.

Helen wobbles out of her bedroom and looks around, "God? Are you calling me?" Through hushed snickering, they intone, "Yes, Helen. Look up. I'm way up high … "

As she lifts her bouffant blue-gray head toward the light, the mischievous little munchkins toss a bed sheet from over the balcony, landing on top of Helen like a make shift ghost costume at Halloween. We often discover Helen zigzagging down the hallway, arms stretched like a zombie, moaning with confused despair trying to find her way to the aid of an adult.

This is the most difficult parenting situation ever—correcting naughty antics while trying to hold back my own sadistic giggles. I could win an Oscar for my acting performance as the parental disciplinarian.

Dinner is always a disaster. I can't quite cook to her standard. I am accustomed to receiving flying food hurled at me with an insult attached regarding the consistency of the mashed potatoes or the pink inside the steak. One evening, while I dodge a spoonful of projectile peas that aren't warm enough for Helen's taste, she looks at my husband and says, "Do you know what name your wife called me today?"

Looking from right to left at my face and back to Helen like a ping-pong match, Tom responds, "What, Grandma?"

Sitting up straighter and pursing her Cruella Deville lips, she responds, "She called me a hooker."

Gulp. The bite I'm currently chewing seems to expand down my wind pipe as I gasp for air. A hooker? Seriously, woman?

Tom glances at me with a follow-my-lead expression, "Kasey, tell Grandma you're sorry for calling her a hooker."

Daggers shoot from my eyes, "What?! Fine. Grandma, I'm sorry I called you a hooker, even though that never happened. I apologize."

Helen gets her revenge. Every weekend, I become her errand-running minion, enslaved by her demands for stool softeners, denture adhesive, hemorrhoid cream, pantyhose, house dresses, and girdles. Why bother with a girdle at 93 years old? No wonder she's such a grump!

Vitamins. Oh, the vitamins. I run all over town looking for specific magic pills. This is self-defeating. Why on earth am

I helping her get supplements that will prolong her life? Am I insane?

Bra shopping.

Kill me now.

Hours are spent at JC Penney walking up and down each section of the store with Helen wearing the bra on the outside of her blouse. She refuses to try on undergarments in the dressing room because she is convinced video cameras are planted inside the mirrors recording her naked breasticles. (Breasticles are what I call boobs that have fallen so low they now resemble testicles in shape, consistency, and location.) Yes, Helen. Because that's what all America wants to see on YouTube: your flapping windsocks.

Off we go, hand in hand, parading for all to see Warner's Wonder-Lifting Bra, Cosmopolitan's Ego Elevator, and even Playtex's Natural Nursing bra. Why on earth do we need to try on a nursing bra?

Black. Beige. White. Peach. Pink. Floral. But never red. Red is only for sluts.

Oh, good grief.

Through the linen section, through the hair salon, around and around the table of men's neckties, and up and down the cases of Timex watches ... just Helen, the very visible bra, and me. Not knowing what else to do, I lift my chin, pull my shoulders back, and wave at the spectators like I'm the Queen of England.

Lesson Learned: Someday, I will also be 93 years old and will need a new bra. Someone please make me read this story again to remind myself to be kind to whomever is forced to take care of me by wiping my old saggy butt and hand-washing my RED, lacey, slutty, push-up bra.

Peeking Buns Preventing Peking Duck

We live in a quiet neighborhood. Sure, there are kids who play ball in the street and the occasional parent yelling for the home-from-college driver to slow down, but nothing much happens here—except the consuming suspicion that the morbidly obese dude who lives five houses down is throwing all-male swingers parties at his house. But besides that, we simply enjoy watching momma ducks waddle their babies over to our lawn to feast on junebugs under the watchful eye of the ancient Chinese grandmother whom my neighbor props in her front yard under an umbrella like a human lawn gnome. As usual, this old woman ignores me as I wave a cheerful greeting, and again I make the mental note that I should bring her some ice cream to keep her cool.

Today would not be that day.

Exhausted from a long day at work, I hobble through the front door lugging as many bags of groceries as I can possibly carry. My only goal is to remove the embedded plastic that painfully digs into my arms as I've taken on more bags than I should in order to eliminate multiple trips to the car. I make my first step into the house when Johnny Cash (my son's scrappy little mutt whose only perfected trick is crapping on my husband's pillow) darts out the door.

This isn't the first or even twentieth time he's gotten loose. The other neighbor, who sells illegal appliances from his garage, just happens to be the city's animal control officer. This man is on a first name basis with Johnny Cash and has placed this mutt in his own version of Folsom County Prison several times, much to the dismay of our credit card that posts the bail.

Okay. Maybe the neighborhood is a bit more bizarre than I care to admit.

The dog immediately spots yellow downy prey but not before a large white momma duck flaps in between them, honking loudly in protest. The chase is on. The baby is in the lead—repeatedly launched a foot ahead by the momma's beak like a tennis ball rolling in rebellion away from the player. Momma duck scurries mere inches from the dog's chompers. Snap! Snap!

I take off after them in hot pursuit.

Down the street we go—the duck honking, the dog snarling, and me yelling, "No, Johnny Cash!" while clomping along in four-inch stilettos and a flirty skirt not meant for long-distance running nor dog-chasing in the wind. We round the corner and dodge traffic on the main road.

The cute college boy vrooms past us in his sports car and witnesses the shenanigans that might turn fatal for any one of us in this mad conga line. He pulls over and joins the chase behind me, although I'm not quite sure which one of us he is trying to save.

Catapulting duckling. Honking momma. Ravenous canine. Hobbling me. College Rescuer. All in hot pursuit of each other down the esplanade. We must have been quite a sight—especially me as my flippy skirt exposes my thong-exposed-cheeks to the coed chasing behind me and the twenty dodging cars that are slowing down to watch the show.

It's the only time in six years I've witnessed the Chinese neighbor look remotely alive. She actually smiles and claps her arthritic hands as I'm guessing she is envisioning the makings of Peking duck for dinner.

Not on my watch, lady.

Lunging in desperation to save the fowl and my bare-buns-and-bunions, I spring forward to grab Johnny Cash's tail. With a yelp from the dog and a thud of my body, I salvage the ducks' lives as the college boy heroically lifts me back to a vertical position and carries my dog back home for me.

I learned many lessons from this bizarre episode:

Lesson Learned from the Duckling: When momma tells you to run, listen! She's trying to keep you safe. This applies to either the dog who's trying to eat you—or when you're sixteen years old and the wolf masquerading himself as a teenage boy's eyes are too hungry for your own good.

Lesson Learned from the Momma Duck: Any mother will risk her own life to protect her baby from the jaws of death, whether you are human, animal, or soon-to-be duck pâté on a cracker.

Lesson Learned from the College Dude: It's okay for a modern day lady to still accept help from a dashing rescuer. After all, I'm pretty sure he was helping out because of the pitty, not the pretty. A girl can pretend though.

Lesson Learned from the Old Chinese Neighbor: I've always wondered what was meant by that laundry commercial for Calgon in the 1970's regarding the "Ancient Chinese Secret". I've figured it out: sit back and cheer on the exciting races life throws *at us.*

And finally ...

Lesson Learned from Yours Truly: The thematic lesson I keep trying to tell myself throughout *all* of my wacky experiences: for the benefit of everyone's retinas and my depleting pride, it's time to start wearing full-bottom panties!

CONCLUSIONS

The Bible says in the third chapter of Ecclesiastes, "There is a time for everything." I believe this. I also believe as women we try to cram too much into a day's work whether the time is right or not. Mostly for fear of letting someone else down and feeling like we won't quite measure up if we aren't spinning eighty-two plates all at once, regardless of how crazy it makes us feel in return.

We run around with a plastered smile on our face and our Super Chick cape heroically flowing behind us while fixing scuffs in shoes with a Sharpie marker, squeezing blobs of ketchup to camouflage anything that remotely tastes vegetable-ish, while volunteering as homeroom mom, soccer coach, Sunday school aficionado, co-worker to the jerk in the next cubicle whom we fantasize about stabbing in the eye with a pencil because we're sick of hearing about his epic weekend trysts, laundry goddess, mothers to children whom we swore would never behave the way they do, and wife to a man who gets turned on just by watching us excavate runaway Cheerios from the inside of our bra.

We will survive this ... with the help of girlfriends who make us giggle just by catching their eye at precisely the right moment and a sexy pair of heels that make us feel a little more Angelina Jolie and a lot less Alice from *The Brady Bunch*. Because someday in time, we *will* miss those grubby little fingers wiggling in desperation for our attention under the bathroom door and kisses that leave behind remnants of grape jelly on our cheek.

And we will have grown and learned a lot of lessons throughout these wacky times.

I think.